READER'S REPORT

READER'S REPORT

ON THE WRITING OF NOVELS

by

CHRISTOPHER DERRICK

LONDON
VICTOR GOLLANCZ LTD
1970

© CHRISTOPHER DERRICK 1969

First published May 1969

Second impression January 1970

575 00266 2

MADE AND PRINTED IN GREAT BRITAIN BY
THE GARDEN CITY PRESS LIMITED
LETCHWORTH, HERTFORDSHIRE

CONTENTS

THE WORK OF A PUBLISHER'S READER

THIS BOOK MAY need to justify its existence. 'The novel' is a subject that has attracted a good deal of attention in recent years, and in any suitable bookshop or library you can find it well and extensively handled by any number of first-class writers. Great novelists have explained their different manners of working; critics have commented in detail upon their individual works; the history and theory of the matter have been elaborated in various ways. What need, what possibility is there of a new approach?

Broadly speaking, you can do three things with a novel. In the first place, you can read it; and in so far as you are simply a reader of novels, you are well catered for. Every week sees the appearance of many new titles; and if you have a problem of choice, the reviewers are there to advise you, not to mention that helpful girl in the library. You can freely and irresponsibly enjoy whatever pleasures and benefits are offered by novels old and new : there's no problem here.

In the second place, you can make the novel an object of intellectual attention, of more or less systematic study. And here again, you are well catered for. After some neglect in the past, the universities now take this subject very seriously; if you aren't a full-time student, there are public lectures and evening classes and correspondence schools, relevant to this branch of literary study. And for all of us, there are biographies and bibliographies and critical studies of every description, histories of the novel, analyses of particular works, theoretical surveys, and so forth. These can be bought or borrowed : if you want to become knowledgeable about the novel, you have no external cause for frustration.

But there's a third possibility. Apart from reading novels and studying them, you can also desire to write them; and here, you may run into difficulties. You may find it hard to get started; you may find it hard to get finished; you may finish your novel and then fail to get it published. This book has its origin in a belief that needs and problems of this third kind are rather inadequately catered for at the present time; and in the further belief that if the aspiring novelist is to be helped at all, the specialised experience of a publisher's reader may well be useful to him.

This is not, therefore, a work of formal criticism or of literary theory; nor does it attempt the illusory task of drawing up a set of rules or instructions, which—if carefully followed—might guarantee success in the art of novel-writing. The programme is humbler and more realistic. For the most part, this book is based upon some fifteen years' experience in the work of a publisher's reader, and it consists essentially of reportage from the field in which practical assessments and recommendations are made; and it is chiefly intended to help those people who aspire to write novels and then to see them published.

To such people, it may be useful in a practical way. If they want their work to see print, they must necessarily hope to please the publisher's reader in the first instance. How does his mind work? What is he looking for? What characteristics—in a typescript submitted for publication—are liable to arouse boredom and irritation in his mind? How are his recommendations made and formulated? Why was *my* novel rejected? In a personal revelation or report that tries to answer such questions, the aspiring novelist may find something of interest.

In a secondary and less practical way, this book may also be useful in offering a new perspective, a reminder that when we speak casually of 'the novel' we are commonly using that expression in a narrow and selective sense. Occasionally at least, the student of literature should remember that it has a very wide reference : it covers a large and complex reality, not having quite the character or shape that might be suggested by most books of criticism.

Some years ago, I was approached by the editor of a continental monthly : he brought forward the flattering suggestion that I should write for his pages a long article—some twelve thousand words—on 'The Novel in Britain Today'. It sounded an attractive assignment, though no large payment was offered : I roughed out a few headings and got down to work.

But as I proceeded, I felt increasingly conscious of a curious hallucinatory feeling, as though I were walking on non-existent ground in a dream-landscape; and this bothered me. In the end, I climbed down and said that I couldn't possibly write the article after all.

What was the difficulty? We all know well enough what kind of article that editor wanted—a long essay, full of generalised interpretations of the time, in which suitable writers and their books were featured prominently—Iris Murdoch, Alan Sillitoe, Graham Greene, Anthony Burgess, whoever else you like to name.

Such articles are often written. But as a publisher's reader, I was the wrong person to do the job. There was a risk of falsity : it would have involved a selective distortion of my own experience—rather as if, in an article about 'London', I had concentrated upon Buckingham Palace, the Tower, the Inns of Court, St Paul's, and the Changing of the Guard. These tourist-attractions are certainly there, but they do not bulk very large in my own total experience of London. What I see, for the most part, is miles and miles of nondescript suburb.

A publisher's reader is, unquestionably, a literary critic. But his normal dwelling is in the suburbs of literature, and even in its slums : he is not the best guide if you want to be taken around and shown the few tourist-attractions, the colourful high-spots, but he's well placed for surveying the city as a whole.

To vary the metaphor, let us compare 'the novel' to an iceberg.

From the deck of a passing ship, we see a great solid mass, rising here and there to a small number of glittering pinnacles. But hidden beneath the water-line of publication, there's another and a much larger mass, dark and gloomy, invisible to the general reader and even to the keen student, known only to publishers and their readers.

That editor wanted an article on the glittering pinnacles: but they weren't what I chiefly saw when—from my distinctive and mostly submerged viewpoint—I surveyed the iceberg. He wasn't interested in 'the novel' as a whole, the novel-as-written, nor even in the novel-as-published: he was concerned with something much smaller and quite untypical, the novel-as-talked-about.

The point is worth stressing, if only for the sake of explaining and justifying this book. It will, necessarily, include approaches and judgments that may seem unexpected or incongruous to those who are concerned with 'the novel' in the narrower, more colourful sense. The dark submerged mass is very different from the glittering pinnacles, and it cannot usefully be discussed in the same terms or criticised by the same standards: an approach that's relevant to the analysis of masterpieces will not usually be helpful to the novelist who's struggling to achieve a pass-mark.

In writing this report on my experiences around and below the water-line, I have the benefit of a comforting but dangerous alibi: I cannot easily be proved wrong, since so much of my subject-matter is not available for public discussion.

It may be useful to give here some account of the life and work of a publisher's reader. Many people seem to look upon this as a glamorous or—at least—a notably interesting occupation; in particular, those who are studying English Literature in the universities will often be found to cherish an ambition in this direction. What experiences will be yours, what daily routine, what responses, when this business of reading manuscripts and reporting upon them has become, wholly or partially, your life's work?

"Publishers' readers seldom, if ever, get the praise they deserve": these are the words of Sir Stanley Unwin, written many years ago; and he went on to quote a most distinguished author's opinion, that in the art of criticism these confidential readers far outshine the public reviewers.

True or false in your own particular case, such words are comforting: you remember them, needing their support as you open this latest parcel and stare dolefully at the huge dog-eared typescript within. Yours is a romantic task, you remind yourself, an exciting one: or so it seems to many envious people outside. Here you are in the very front line of literature, shaping the moment of decision, exercising behind the throne the power of an *éminence grise*. "Shall we let this fellow live?" asks the publisher: your lips are pursed, you shake your head, and the wretched man is led away to oblivion. Alternatively, you give a cautious provisional nod, and a destiny is launched that will culminate in fireworks and champagne and honorary doctorates. "Yes," you will tell your grandchildren, "she's required reading now in all your colleges. But I found her, I made her; I detected her promise when she was starving unrecognised in a garret, unable to afford even a new ribbon for her typewriter."

Cheered by these conceited imaginings, with your hope rising once again after a thousand disappointments, you riffle through the pages before you. In a physical sense at least, the thing appears to be readable. That typewriter-ribbon was bought and used, at whatever cost in privation: you will not be grappling this time with a reappearance of that most hellish and hateful author, the one who submits a four-inch pile of slithery onion-skin paper, invisibly typed, unnumbered, unfastened; all bursting out from a broken cardboard box.

The publisher's letter explains that this is a first novel, that the author is young and female and keen and willing to take advice, and that the agent recommends her and her work very warmly indeed: as well he may. And so you mobilise the full power of your optimism. This may be a day of golden discovery: the great mouldering haystack of mediocre writing may now be on the point of yielding up another of its rare golden needles. You lay out notebook and ballpoint and perhaps a glass of anaesthetic, and you settle down to read.

You have to go carefully. Within the high craft and priesthood of criticism, there are many mansions : this particular task makes its own demands upon you, distinct from those made upon the academic critic or the reviewer. For one thing, you have to be broad-minded in a rather exceptional degree, catholic in your tastes : you must be able and willing to recognise successful achievement in a wide variety of literary kinds, including some that are seldom taken seriously by other critics. This present typescript may well reveal itself unmistakably, within the first ten pages, as a sentimental novelette for silly adolescents; whereas you yourself are naturally wise and mature, dwelling habitually upon the cultural heights. In such a case, your personal response will hardly be to the point. There are a great many silly adolescents; they seem to have money nowadays; they constitute a market that your publisher may wish to exploit. If you want to be generally useful as a literary adviser, you must be prepared in this case to think yourself back into that teenage mind, to receive the book on its own terms, and then judge it by relevant standards. And your next parcel may contain a treatise on theology.

This necessary tolerance, this adaptability of your response, has a vertical dimension as well. Apart from that variety in literary *genres,* your professional reading will vary in mere merit, to a degree not experienced—and hardly to be imagined—by critics who work in other fields. You handle best-selling mastery today, near-illiteracy tomorrow.

In this, you are alone. The book-reviewer, writing in the public press, handles nothing that has not already been judged publishable, by however depraved a standard : the academic critic lives in even greater luxury, needing only to consider such books as have clear value and importance. Your case is less fortunate. From time to time you are in stimulating company; from time to time you make discoveries. But these are exceptional cases.

For the most part, a publisher's reader is a man paid to read unreadable books; it is his disheartening task to conduct an examination in which most of the candidates will fail, to search a haystack in which the needles are few.

It is a sad situation, arising naturally from the competitive nature of publishing and from the widespread delusion that anybody can write. And it creates a particular danger: your standards can easily become debauched. After reading six typescripts in a row, all of them flat and dead, you may be tempted to hail the seventh author as a genius if he shows even the slightest degree of life and power. If only for this reason, if only as a necessary insurance, you must vary your reading: regularly, you must lay your work aside and read something wonderfully and unquestionably good—even without payment.

This maintenance of your standards and your sense of proportion is part of the responsibility that you owe to your publisher—a notably concrete responsibility, without parallel in other kinds of criticism. The academic critic or the reviewer is responsible to truth and to his own reputation: if he misses the point grossly and offers a foolish judgment, there will be no bones broken. He is not called upon to answer any specific question in decisive practical terms: he will not be held to account for his opinions.

But you, advising a publisher on his choice of titles, are in a position more exacting and possibly more embarrassing. Recommend this particular novel, and you will be inviting some personal friends of yours to stake a very considerable sum of money upon an unknown horse, running in a painfully competitive race. You will not be disposed to make any such recommendation lightly; on the other hand, you have heard harrowing tales of chances missed by too much caution. How many masterpieces, now acknowledged, went circulating around in their early days from one publishing house to another, turned down repeatedly, with dismissive comment from just such people as yourself! Sometimes you lie awake at night and worry about it. It is bad enough to be responsible for selling the firm another lead balloon; it is much worse, surely, to go on record as the timid and negative fellow who let a fat pigeon get away.

And so you press on in some anxiety, determined to do more than justice to this poor girl who now lies at your mercy. Already, by page 43 or thereabouts, you know in your secret heart that it won't do : the imitative flatness of her mind has become manifest, the poverty of her imagination, the clumsiness of her structural contrivance, the crude approximation of her language. But you must not give up. The book may improve surprisingly in the last three chapters; it may prove a case, if not for acceptance, at least for active encouragement; or it may be striving towards some new mode of expression, so alien to your preconceptions that it seems at first like mere incompetence. The author must have the benefit of any possible doubt.

And if your negative response is total, it must therefore be suspect. No book can be wholly bad, with no merit at all : there is at least one human being, your equal before God and the law, in whose eyes it stands there as a thing achieved and perfect, a dream made concrete, a darling child. This vision of the book may seem grossly implausible to you; but you must make the effort, and try to see it in those terms, through the author's satisfied eyes. Until on this experimental basis you have made the vision your own, you cannot possibly assess its validity.

Even this book, therefore, needs to be treated with respect. Finish it punctiliously, without skipping; then lay it aside, and go over it in memory, and consult and elaborate your notes. Then sleep on it.

An exacting and responsible kind of critical attention; and you may come to resent its continual deployment upon objects that are for the most part, when all's said and done, unworthy of it. But you will have your revenge next morning, when you come to type your report—accurate description in the first place, literary and commercial evaluation in the second, with a precise recommendation to conclude. This kind of critical writing has the unique character of being wholly confidential; only a few people will ever read it, friends who know you all too well, so that you are under slight temptation to display your cleverness and erudition as reviewers sometimes do. And you are in a blessed state of freedom : you can forget about libel, you can ignore the conventional politenesses of public discourse, you can say what you *really* think.

Back, therefore, this typescript must go, to the obscurity of its origin. It may find another publisher, more kindly disposed towards it : more probably—like the next, like the one after— it is destined never to take its place in the emerging pattern of present-day literature. It is already a part of that total reality that we call 'the novel', but it will stay below the water-line : people on passing ships won't suspect its existence, and it's far indeed from the glittering pinnacles where the critic-birds hover and swoop and screech.

And so it goes on : you suspect, sometimes, that this endless writing of dismissive reports does some kind of harm to your soul. But then, from time to time, without warning, the gods send down your reward and your justification. It may seem an ordinary thing to begin with, and you approach it with no particular expectation; but as you read it your attention heightens, and you find the contrived optimism of your daily routine blossoming slowly into real hope and real excitement. Your report is positive this time, more pleasant to write, though you always include some note of caution : if books are never wholly bad, they are seldom wholly perfect, and you offer no exaggerated promises. The publisher agrees, your advice is taken : slowly, the wheels start to turn, with yourself marginally involved at various stages —talking to the author, advising on the necessary revision, approving the finished job, perhaps writing the blurb.

And then, one day, there will be a great popping of flashbulbs and corks, a launching, a celebration and delight of achievement. Author and publisher will bask together in well-deserved lime-light : you will sit back in the shadows, your name not publicised. It was small but crucial, the part that you played in the enter-prise : if the author hadn't succeeded in pleasing you first of all,

15

he would have had small opportunity of pleasing the critics and the public.

Unobtrusively, you slip away from that launching party : there are several typescripts waiting for you at home, a grey burden (in all probability) for the morning. But this latest episode has given you a sense of achievement, a midwife's pleasure in vicarious motherhood : the batteries of your hope are recharged and brimming over, and you can hardly wait to begin.

Upon such a pattern of experience—somewhat less concentrated in practice, somewhat less colourful—this book is founded. May it prove helpful, in mitigating—or at least in explaining— the bitter blows of rejection and failure.

It should be stressed, perhaps, that this is one man's view of the matter : it contains idiosyncrasies and limitations. Ideally, one would like to see the publisher's reader as an utterly objective and perfect critic, infallible in his judgments : if this were possible, the publisher would only need to do what he was told, and his work would be much easier and much less interesting. In fact, this is not the case. There are no infallible critics; and if there were, they could hardly be persuaded to pass their working lives in the slummy and suburban regions of literature. They would look for some grander destiny.

As a critic, in the high academic sense of the word, the publisher's reader is therefore likely to be a somewhat limited fellow. He must not esteem himself too highly. The publisher does not submit to his judgment in humble fashion, as a student of literature might submit to the judgment of some august senior critic, wide in his erudition, ripe in his discernment. The whole business can be seen in more pedestrian terms. If in one sense he's a a critic, the publisher's reader is in another sense a mere member of the public, qualified only by the fact that his responses are clearcut and articulate : in sending him some typescript for comment, the publisher is—so to speak—trying it on the dog.

And the dog's reaction will not always be trustworthy. In some degree, the publisher will trust his judgment : if an opinion is worth paying for, it needs to have some kind of probable rightness. But it may need interpretation. The reader will have blind spots, and various bees will buzz in his individual bonnet : knowing him of old, the publisher will be able to make allowance for these. In any case that's marginal or otherwise interesting, he will take another opinion or perhaps several.

Then, if he decides to reject this particular book, another publisher may accept it eagerly. Requirements vary; the market changes; tastes differ. There is no single process of authoritative judgment.

The point is that the opinions offered in this book are highly personal : they do not reflect the editorial policy of any particular publishing house, nor yet the general habit of mind that prevails among publishers. They represent nothing more than the personal conclusions—and even the personal prejudices— of one who has spent many years in close attention to the phenomena and mechanisms of literary failure and success. And 'success', in this context, means for the most part mere publishability : we are not concerned with the heights. Every publisher would like to father a new twentieth-century classic, and every reader would like to have the credit of making some thumping discovery; but for reasons of mere economics, the routine of the game is more pedestrian.

With the difference between greatness and near-greatness, therefore, this book will hardly be concerned at all. Its ideal reader is the aspiring novelist who has so far failed to achieve publication, and who wonders why.

CHAPTER ONE

THE POSSIBLE NOVELIST

A GREAT MANY PEOPLE desire to write novels. For some, there's no difficulty at all. They just get down to it—as a full-time occupation in some cases, but more usually in whatever odd moments are left over from their job or the housekeeping. The typewriter clatters, or the pen skims easily : soon it's finished, a new novel, a thing perfect and complete in its author's eyes at least.

And this easy writing may, quite conceivably, be followed by easy selling : there's nothing very extraordinary in a new writer's first novel being accepted by the first publisher who sees it. A contract will be signed, proofs will be corrected, advance copies will be looked upon with amazement and delight : soon the great day of publication will arrive, with congratulations all round. Fame and money will come rolling in.

Such things can happen. People have been prophesying the death of the novel for many years, but it seems to be alive and vigorous none the less, still a sound proposition for the publisher and the author as well. The market is wide open : in order to get your novel published, it is not in the least necessary that you should have an established name, or be in a position to pull influence. And in a sense, there is nothing very difficult about writing a novel. The exercise certainly calls for a number of particular gifts, but these are fairly widespread, not the preserve of a sophisticated minority. You may well have them, and there's no reason at all why you shouldn't be able to put them into successful practice.

All this needs to be said and remembered. None the less, the ugly fact remains that this is a field in which failure and disappointment are the rule rather than the exception. It is easy and pleasant to dream of being a successful novelist, but those who try to put this dream into practice tend—for the most part—to run into serious difficulties. In the first place, many of them find it almost impossible to get started. They sit and look at the blank paper before them, and they cudgel their brains and bite their nails and stare out of the window, but nothing *comes*. Secondly, if they do manage to get started, the thing is all too likely to peter out lamely after a few pages or chapters have been drafted. Finally, where a novel does manage to get itself completed—whether easily or with tremendous effort—there's no certainty at all that it's going to be published. It may go the rounds from one publishing house to another, returned always with a short polite letter of rejection, until the author loses heart and decides to waste no more postage-money on it.

These three predicaments are suffered very widely: the world is full of frustrated and disappointed novelists. It is the purpose of this book to give them some help and relief, in so far as my own experience—chiefly as a publisher's reader, but in other and related fields as well—may render this possible.

Looking back through the file of his reports, accumulated over many years, the publisher's reader will feel a certain sadness and even a vague irrational sense of guilt. This file of his constitutes the only surviving monument to countless efforts that were wholly in vain, hopes that were unrealistic from the start, vocations to the novelist's trade that were plainly and grossly mistaken; and it was his hand that wielded the chopper. Here and there, he will catch the name of some book that did well and was perhaps his own discovery: there will be a few best-sellers among them, many novels that enjoyed a sound modest useful kind of success, and some that succeeded in a specialised way, being unknown to the public at large but deeply appreciated by a keen few. But the majority of his reports will be negative, referring to books that never had much chance: it is sad to reflect that each one of them—here dismissed in a few sharp critical sentences that weren't for publication—represents the heart's blood of some would-be novelist, his sweat and dedication over many agonising and hopeful months.

Conscious of the waste and pathos of all this, he may develop a slightly jaundiced and negative attitude to the whole matter : if you tell him that you hope to write novels and would be grateful for his advice, you may well be given advice of an unwelcome kind, firmly discouraging and deterrent. "Don't do it!" he may reply. "Don't invest your time and your emotional capital in an enterprise which—statistically speaking—offers you so slender a chance of success!"

This will of course be miserable and chicken-hearted advice, all too characteristic of a man who spends most of his time in the dispiriting land of failure : it is to be hoped that you treat it with the contempt that it so richly deserves. Even so, there is something to be gained by an occasional exercise in radical scepticism and the scrutiny of motivations. Do you *really* want to write? Do you really want to write *novels*? And what makes you think you're well qualified to do it?

Human motivations are always obscure, and the desire to write —or the desire to be a writer, which isn't quite the same thing— is as mysterious as any. It lies wide open to cynical interpretation and comment, and this will seldom be wholly mistaken. For all but the best of us, vanity will certainly come into the picture : we aspire to the status and dignity that is still accorded to the writer.

It may be true, as some people suggest, that the printed word has had its day : we may be moving into a post-literate society, one that will be increasingly governed and fed by the visual image, the heard sound, the visceral or kinaesthetic experience, and less and less by books of any kind. This may be what's happening; but if so, the process hasn't gone very far yet, and it still remains true that in our society the writer—like 'the artist' in any mode—is a highly-regarded figure. In many contexts, the word 'writer' is almost synonymous with the word 'intellectual' : it suggests membership in the intelligentsia, a kind of leadership in connection with the ideas and developments and trends of one's society, almost a kind of priesthood. Around the literary man, there still hangs an aura of separateness and Bohemian romance; introduce yourself to some casual party-acquaintance as 'a writer', and you will evoke an immediate response of interest and curiosity, such as would not be given to any industrialist or civil servant. ("*How* interesting! What do you write? How do you get your ideas? You know, I've *always* wanted to be a writer myself!")

All this is sweet, and a man is not to be blamed very seriously if, in mere vanity, he deeply fancies a literary image of himself.

Such an image will appeal also to his desire for freedom or independence. It is obvious enough that the professional writer doesn't have to clock in at any factory or office : he is his own master, he works for himself alone and at his own pace, he is independent of routine and location and other people's orders. We see him going off to that cottage in Dorset (roses over the door, hollyhocks in the garden, no problems apart from the amusingly primitive sanitation and the fact that Mrs Drudge the housekeeper *will* keep on talking, bless her); and we see him tapping away, pipe in mouth—a free happy man, and creative as few of us can be.

A charming picture indeed, and there's more to it than that. We see him going off to London in a few weeks' time, with that typescript stuffed clumsily into a big dirty old envelope; and he'll hand it over in the course of the delicious lunch that his publisher will buy for him at the Garrick—*tournedos Rossini*, no doubt, with a bottle of Chateauneuf du Pape. Then he'll be off on his travels : Manhattan to begin with, another lunch with another publisher, and the odd party, with celebrities crowded and jabbering together in some mink-lined gin-sodden apartment; then Montego Bay, Acapulco, the Pacific, and suddenly the tide of creation will start running again and he'll have to settle unexpectedly for a while, tapping away once more in some veranda'd house, fretted and crumbling, a relic of French imperialism, while the breakers thunder·on the distant coral reef.

There are novelists who live like this. If you want to be one of them, you must arrange to have both brilliance and facility to some *genre* that's widely acceptable; or alternatively, to have private means. The average writer of books makes, from his writing, rather less than the salary commonly paid to a school-leaving copy-typist. He may find it possible to live where he chooses and work to his own schedule : only exceptionally will his writing enable him to live high, wide, and handsome.

And it will be hard work. A literary image of oneself can appeal realistically to one's vanity and (in some degree) to one's desire for freedom, but it cannot honestly appeal to one's laziness. Some people find it possible to write at high speed and effort-lessly : more usually, if high speed is achieved, it is only achieved at the expense of vast effort and a heavy drain on the writer's nerves. (It is reported that Simenon writes and revises each of his stories within a period that seldom exceeds a fortnight; but it's a hectic fortnight, and he has to have a medical check-up before and afterwards.) Conversely, you may manage to conserve your energies and write your novel in an easy restful kind of way; but in this case, it may take an impossibly long time to write, and it's very likely to go off the boil and die on your hands.

For most writers, the process is long-drawn-out as well as arduous : it tends to be a burden, a boring agony, a drain on the nerves. "Whenever I am writing, I am physically ill," said Dostoievsky. "Sometimes I can't make out why my arms don't fall off my body with weariness, or why my brains don't turn to porridge" : thus Flaubert recorded the joys of the literary life.

None the less, many people seem to believe that the writer has an easy time of it, as compared (say) with the business man. This may be partly because his work isn't all done at his desk, and is —to some extent—a matter of day-dreaming and cogitation. "Reverie is the groundwork ·of the creative imagination," said Somerset Maugham; "it is the privilege of the artist that with him it is not as with other men an escape from reality, but the means by which he accedes to it." True enough, but misleading if we infer that the writer's life is essentially one of pipe-smoking meditation, an easy thinking of beautiful thoughts. In a loose sense, we can say that the novelist is 'working'—or can be—when he's leaning on a gate and watching the sunset, or rioting in some hellish night-spot in Tangier, or conducting a fruitfully agonising love-affair. In all such circumstances, he may well be gathering or marshalling his material. None the less, his actual work will almost certainly be *work*, in the most grievous sense of the word, and hard work in every sense but the physical : each sentence will have to be hammered out in blood and tears.

There is, then, nothing very easy about the life and work of the writer, and it is certainly not particularly rewarding in any financial way. A man who's intelligent and energetic enough to write a tolerable novel will have before him many alternative ways of earning whatever money he needs : most of these will be more rewarding, in terms of the time and effort invested, and nearly all will be more certain.

The point needs to be stressed. Novel writing is not a good way of getting money. From time to time one meets somebody who would not think of writing a novel in the ordinary course of things, but has suddenly resolved to write one now, simply because a domestic crisis—or something of that kind—has inflicted upon him an unexpected necessity of finding two hundred pounds rather quickly. He may succeed : great work has sometimes been produced under that kind of pressure, with the telephone cut off and the broker's men in the house. But the odds, the statistics are against him : he would not be acting very much more imprudently if he relied upon a solid and careful investment in one of the smaller football pools. Either course of action *might* lead to an easing of his problems; but each has the character of a gamble, and will not be relied upon by a prudent man in urgent need of money.

The odds, although they are certainly adverse, cannot be precisely known. The statistics of publishing are, of course, a matter of public record : during 1967, there were 2259 new novels published in Great Britain and 1981 in the United States. But these constitute the fortunate minority, and there is no assessing the number of their unsuccessful contemporaries and competitors. One can say with confidence, however, that if this were only known, it would prove to be a much larger number. All publishers reject most of the novels submitted to them : most reader's reports are negative. This book is based chiefly upon a very extensive file of such reports covering a period of some fifteen years, and referring only to such manuscripts as had already survived a first coarse filtering, a preliminary process of weeding out; and of these reports, only about 16 per cent are positive, implying some kind of recommendation, usually guarded or qualified in one way or another. The rave report—"Grab this without fail, and publish it as it stands!"—occurs very seldom indeed; and for a variety of reasons, even a favourable report is by no means always followed by publication. In about 58 per cent of cases, a flat rejection is recommended with no doubt or qualification at all, and advice of this kind is usually taken; while the remaining 26 per cent of these reports express intermediate judgments of one kind or another. (The percentage rate of recommendation, and of publication too, is considerably higher in the field of non-fiction.)

These gloomy figures will not deter a spirited and confident author, and it is not intended that they should. "The race is not to the swift, nor the battle to the strong" : the game is essentially competitive, and good work only comes into existence against an extensive background of relative failure. There has to be 'prentice work, there have to be fumblings and experiments and false starts; there will only be needles if the haystack is big, and the aspiring novelist—if he has the right stuff in him—will be positively put on his mettle by the challenge and adversity of the fight.

None the less, there are some people to whom advice of a deterrent kind can properly be given. In particular, it seems unwise to attempt the serious practice of an art that you don't love. The writer, as such, is a person who handles the language : his dealings are with words and sentences, with patterns and structures that are verbal. He needs to care about these things : his heart cannot be wholly given to his subject-matter, the splendid things that he's going to say. W. H. Auden puts the point well : "A poet has to woo, not only his own Muse but also Dame Philology, and, for the beginner, the latter is the more important. As a rule, the sign that a beginner has a genuine original talent is that he is more interested in playing with words than in saying something original." In some degree, this applies to all writers, not only to poets : the practitioner of any skill needs to be somewhat in love with the stuff he handles.

An astonishing number of writers fail, simply because they handle the language with indifference or contempt : they do not look with love, or even with mere businesslike attention, or perhaps even at all, upon the individual sentences that they write, the individual words that they choose. The consequences are usually disastrous. It is not merely that such writers fail to satisfy some lofty academic criterion of literary elegance : their books simply don't function, they aren't readable. At the best, they create their desired effects in weak and mushy fashion, and are therefore unlikely to hold the attention of any voluntary reader; at the frequently-occurring worst, they are simply hard to construe. One can't puzzle out what the sentences are supposed to mean.

Obscurity is often justified, of course, though rather less often than is supposed by a number of anxiously progressive writers; but the kind of obscurity that arises from a merely slipshod handling of the language is not likely to be forgivable. It's one thing to fail, gallantly, in the attempt to communicate something very difficult : it's quite another to fail ignobly, because you weren't interested in the materials and processes that are involved in the art of verbal communication.

The aspiring writer needs, therefore, to have some kind of practical interest in the actual business of writing. He doesn't need to study it theoretically, but he needs to care about it : in any context, his teeth should be set on edge by the subtly wrong word, the ill-made sentence. His standards may or may not be those of the schoolmaster, the academic precisian, the literary pedant : his own problem may quite possibly be soluble only by methods that will shock the older generation's idea of 'good writing'. Let him go ahead and solve it if he can; but in so far as he is trying to forge a new instrument, a new idiom, his need to care will be all the greater. The current state of literary and linguistic flux, the current challenging of classical and familiar idioms, does not in any way diminish the writer's need to care about his medium : very much the reverse.

The point may seem a shade obvious. But if it were more widely and deeply appreciated, there would be fewer dreary and fruitless burdens inflicted upon the publisher's reader.

Any alleged vocation to the writer's craft must, then, be looked upon with some suspicion unless it is accompanied by some degree of concern and even passion about words and sentences. Where this habit of mind doesn't come naturally, it can perhaps be worked up by effort; but where it altogether fails to exist, the person concerned might do best to take up some other occupation. One doesn't have to be a writer.

And if one is going to be a writer, it doesn't at all follow that one has to write novels. Here again, as with writing in general, there is some danger that adventitious circumstances may generate what—among the monks and Jesuits—would be called 'a false vocation'. The qualifications that you need if you're to write a publishable novel are not particularly rare, but they are not universal : your own gifts, and even your own half-conscious desires, may actually pull you in quite another direction, towards some quite different sort of writing. Even so, 'the novel' will probably attract you like a powerful magnet : you'll determine to write one, regardless. There won't be anything wicked about such a determination, and your attempt will not necessarily be doomed to failure; none the less, it's as well to be forewarned about the difficulties you will make for yourself if, on these lines, you establish a conflict between your natural leanings and your present intention.

The problem arises chiefly because of a certain primacy which most of us still accord to the novel, as against all other kinds of literary work. Novel-writing is, we feel, the typical or central activity of the man of letters: introduce yourself to somebody as 'a writer', and more often than not, you'll find the assumption made at once that you must be a novelist. "Oh, you're a *writer*! Let's see, which of your novels have I read? Just remind me of the titles . . ." Or get talking to some young man who's just down from the university and proposes to embark upon a literary life. His ambitions are complex: he intends to be a poet, a critic, a broadcaster, a lecturer, and so forth. But he'll be very likely to look upon these activities as peripheral: at the centre of his ambitious heart, he'll commonly be thinking of the novels he's going to write.

"The dominant literary form of an age has its dangers as well as its rewards," writes Professor Kathleen Tillotson. "It tends to attract talents, especially minor talents, that in other ages would have found other media or perhaps not literary media at all." This is very true of the novel today; the publisher's reader is constantly handling manuscripts by people who (it seems) chose the novel-form not because their gifts or even their desires prompted them in that direction, but merely because the novel is the largest, the most obvious and central item in today's literary landscape. Born into the eighteenth century, these same people would have written pastoral or satirical poetry in heroic couplets; born two centuries earlier still, they would have written sonnet-sequences about love. Born into our time, they seize upon the novel, instinctively and (in a great many cases) unwisely.

By all means decide to write novels. But let this be a positive choice, made on its merits as seen by yourself: don't just drift into it because you wanted, in general, 'to write', but couldn't find any other form or medium that seemed to lie within your powers. Don't choose the novel as a soft option : it isn't. It may appear to be a soft option because it need not be based upon anything wider than your own experience of life; whereas most other kinds of writing call for specialised knowledge, for facts, for research, and all manner of tedious drudgery. Be warned! The novel also involves drudgery; and at some stage you'll wish desperately that it could emerge from some nice cool file of fact, industriously compiled and neatly disposed, instead of emerging (as it must) from the hot tumult and exhaustion of the poor battered old head.

In a rock-bottom sense, we are all possible novelists : we've all been to school and learnt to write, we can all afford a ball-point and some rough paper, we all have some experience of people and life, and the story-telling instinct is no rare thing. But not all of us are probable novelists.

What are the good signs, what are the marks of a true vocation to the practice of this particular art? Apart from the writer's basic concern for language, what qualifications does the novelist need?

Cautiously, remembering that all such rules have exceptions, we can suggest five separate answers to any question of that kind, five separate talents or gifts that you'll need to have if that novel of yours is to be a sound one. You may perhaps be able to compensate for a certain weakness in one of them by great strength in the other four; but this easy-going principle is not to be pressed very far.

In the first place, the novelist needs to have staying-power. Temperamentally, he must be able to do a great deal of sustained work over a long period; he must be able to keep at it in sunny moods and black, not relying upon flash-in-the-pan enthusiasm.

Some people talk airily about 'writing a book', as if it were something that could be dashed off in a moment. This is not so : quite apart from the inventive or imaginative part of the task, the mere *writing* of a full-length book is a laborious thing. Try this experiment. Take typewriter or pen, as you choose, and write or copy any old rubbish until your hands get tired or your head starts to buzz. Then count the words that you've written; then try to work out an idea of the head-buzzing and the hand-ache that will be involved in the mere transcription of a full-length book, which will probably be more than seventy thousand words long. Then remember that your novel will almost certainly need to be written out several times—in its entirety—before it's fit for publication. You will find yourself sobered and daunted by this experiment.

This burdensome fact—that writing is hard work—has already been mentioned. It is often brought forcibly to the attention of the publisher's reader. Time and time again, he comes across some novel that would be perfectly publishable, if only the author could be persuaded to submit it to one or two further and total re-writings. Advice to this effect is seldom welcome. The author would be glad enough to revise this passage or that, or to undertake the easy armchair task of general tinkering or polishing in detail; but having already done such a fearsome amount of tapping or scribbling, he doesn't want to go back to his desk and a new start. With that extra bit of staying-power, he'd be home and dry: as things are, his novel is half-raw and uneatable.

In the second place, the novelist needs to care about people. This does not mean that he has to be a good and charitable man : Arnold Bennett was talking sentimental nonsense when he said that the essential characteristic of the good novelist was "a Christ-like, all-embracing compassion". That's as may be : you can be an absolute bitch or bastard, and none the worse a novelist for that.

The thing required is a habit of fascinated attention to the human individual. "The dramatist need not understand people," said Eliot, "but he must be exceptionally aware of them." That goes for the novelist too; and since we can't give an equal amount of attention to everything, this kind of awareness will often involve a kind of irresponsibility—personal, social, moral.

"Don't go in for politics," said Gide, "and hardly ever read the newspaper; but do not lose a chance of talking politics with no matter whom : it tells you nothing about public affairs, but it admirably informs you about people's characters."

The born novelist cares about people, but in an irresponsible and even predatory way : he wants to suck their blood, he wants to make use of them. Like the lawyer, he feeds upon their troubles; like the press photographer, he dashes to the scene of disaster—not because he wants to do something in the way of relief and remedy, but rather because he finds there his raw material, his scope, his chance of securing some lovely disgusting printable picture, such as will first nourish his own greedy mind, and will then forward his work and his career and his popularity and his royalty-account.

It is in this kind of sense—a morally questionable sense, obviously—that a novelist needs to care about people. There are higher kinds of caring: compassion, involvement, charity. But with these, the novelist—as such—is much less concerned. Such habits of the mind and heart may well determine the character of his work : they may cause him to write novels of one kind rather than another. But they will contribute little or nothing to the quality of his work : he can get by without them, and even be a brilliant success. Malevolence and cruelty can even contribute to this happy outcome. But he will certainly not get by if his response to the human individual is one of boredom and indifference.

In the third place, the novelist needs a habitual particularity of attention. He should be interested in the isolated case, the unique happening, rather than in general abstractions and broad principles. He needn't care twopence for 'humanity', but he should care furiously about Tom, and Dick, and Harry. When people and places and objects and events are in question, his mind should naturally gravitate towards their differences rather than their resemblances : he should be obsessed by the unique and astonishing quality that resides in everybody and every-thing. If he's interested at all in generalisations and sweeping theories, he keeps all that in a quite separate part of his mind : his professional concern is with the particular, the concrete, the actual and immediate. He will tend not to be a theorist, a partisan, a preacher, or at least not explicitly : his novels may well contain some philosophical message or moral lesson for the world, but only because they reveal his own mind, the manner of his consciousness, and never because he set out to inform or exhort. If philosophy interests him at all, his natural sympathy will be with the nominalists and the existentialists.

The failure of many novels can be diagnosed in terms of a tendency in their authors' minds to generality of attention, a lack of interest in the particular, in the here and now, in this man and that place, in the unique moment and the unrepeatable happening.

In the fourth place, the novelist needs to have—and to use— the gifts needed for large-scale structural engineering in words : at the very least, he must be aware of such problems. A novel has two aspects : it is not only *logos* (a thing said) but also *poiema* (a thing made), and it needs to have a shape, a pattern, a soundly-made structure that can carry the load put upon it. The novelist is, among other things, a craftsman or maker: there must be something in him which, if his life had turned out differently, would have qualified him to design vast bridges, able to withstand hurricanes and heavy loads as well as to please the eye.

An astonishing number of novels fail in this respect. Often the author has failed to solve his structural problems : nearly as often, and more disconcertingly, he doesn't seem to have noticed that such problems arise. Time and time again, therefore, the publisher's reader finds himself blaming a book's failure on to its poor bone-structure : the meat is good, but it droops and sags.

The novelist's fifth and last qualification is of a simple but embarrassing nature. He may work untiringly; he may be abundantly interested in people, and in the right kind of way; he may have a lovely sharp spiky particularity of interest, he may be soundly aware of structural problems and subtly clever

at dealing with them. Even so, his novel may be quite unpublishable, for no reason at all except that its author isn't a very
interesting person.

If this is the case, it's hard to see what can be done about it.
We aren't all interesting; we aren't all good company, and a
man who writes a novel is (in effect) inviting other people to
share the close intimacy of his mind over a long period. These
other people may lose interest, simply because—although very
good and worthy and clever—he is poor company, a dull dog,
something of a bore. A novelist needs to have a mind that's lively
and interesting in one way or another; and this is perhaps the
most crucial point of all. Blessed with a mind of that kind, a
novelist can get away with almost anything; in the absence of
such a mind, his book will be dead, even though it may seem to
be without identifiable faults and weaknesses.

It would be unkind to harp on this rather obvious point,
which plainly doesn't concern the present reader of this book.
But it needs to be mentioned, if only to explain an otherwise
unaccountable kind of silence that occurs from time to time.
"What was *wrong* with my novel? Please tell me, so that I can
do better next time!" Faced with such a question, a publisher
will sometimes change the subject with whatever tact he
possesses; or he may turn red and mumble something vague. It
will not always be wise to press the point: silence may be the
kindest thing all round.

The ugly fact is that a great many novels fail to make the
grade only because they were written by dull and limited people.
There's nothing exactly *wrong* with them, but . . .

Here, then, we have five qualifications, five determining
factors: taken together, they add up to what we may call 'the
creative imagination', as this vague expression can be applied
to the possible novelist. They also add up, no doubt, to a portrait
of yourself.

There's a terrible amount of work ahead of you. Face this,
organise your time, and get down to it. As a publisher's reader,

I have every desire and incentive to give you encouragement and help. For the sake of my bank balance, I want a great many novels to be written and submitted; for the sake of my day-to-day comfort, I want them to be tolerable reading at least; and for the sake of my reputation and pride, I hope one day to discover a masterpiece. It may be yours.

CHAPTER TWO

ABSOLUTE BEGINNERS

Y OU FEEL SURE, then, that you have some kind of need or desire or vocation to write a novel. It's there within you, and it's going to be good. There's only the problem of getting it out of your head and on to the paper that you possess in such virginal quantities.

The first thing necessary is to make an actual start. The world is full of people who were going to be novelists one day, but somehow never got around to it : in order to escape from their sad condition, you need to break the ice and jump in. But you may find this difficult. Time, materials, and a place for writing are all comfortably at your disposal : you type "Chapter I" at the top of your first sheet, and you get stuck precisely there.

The difficulty may be only temporary : you may experience —before long—a sudden melting of the ice, a sudden breaking up of the log-jam, and then find yourself galloping ahead in all fluency and confidence. But this may obstinately refuse to happen; and if after repeated attempts you still find yourself staring hopelessly at paper that's still virginal, you may be tempted to conclude that your dream of writing a novel was quite unrealistic and had better be dropped.

It may be so : not everybody is called and equipped to become a novelist. But you should not despair too soon : the fact that you experience this difficulty in getting started is not, by itself, a proof of anything at all. Even the most successful writers are liable to suffer, at times, from what might be called Author's Constipation. "Now about this book . . . How am I to begin it? And what is it to be? I feel no great impulse; no fever; only a great pressure of difficulty. Why write it then? Why write at all?"

34

These are the despondent words of Virginia Woolf : many other great novelists have written in similar terms.

If you find yourself trapped in this predicament, there are two things that you should bear in mind. The first is the fact that fiction-writing is—for you, at this stage—a new and unfamiliar kind of activity. In launching straight out into a novel, you may be attempting too much, too soon : you may be trying to run before you can walk. The second is the possibility that you may be approaching the job in an unsuitable way; you may be under some kind of misapprehension about how novels are actually made, and even about the whole nature of the creative process.

Give yourself the benefit of the doubt : explore each of these two aspects of the matter, and thoroughly, before you conclude that God didn't mean you to be a novelist.

Bear in mind, to begin with, the possibility that you may need to undertake a certain amount of training. With the other public arts, we take this for granted. The student pianist may look forward to his first recital at the Festival Hall or the Lincoln Center : he knows very well, however, that this day won't come quickly or easily, and that there will first have to be many long years of study and practice, with endless scales and exercises that won't in themselves be worth listening to.

But the corresponding fact about writing is easily overlooked. Having been to school, we can all 'write' : countless people therefore expect their 'prentice work to be publishable, and are too easily discouraged when it's proved otherwise. They should have attended, in all patience, to their scales and exercises.

Suspecting this, many people try to get their hand in, and acquire the basic skills of fiction-writing, by writing short stories —with the idea that after this apprenticeship, they can then move on to their real ambition, the novel. It seems a good idea. The short story (they think) is like a novel but smaller; it can be written more quickly; it represents a more modest initial investment of one's time and energy. Would it not be reasonable, then, if the aspiring novelist wrote a number of short stories by way of 'prentice work? Could these not constitute his scales and exercises? And then, when some of them have been rejected and others published, he will have gained a good deal of useful experience: he will have discovered the lines along which his larger work should develop, if it is to prove acceptable.

Any kind of literary experience is, of course, useful for any kind of writer; and there's a lot to be said for writing short stories. None the less, two fallacies are involved in this particular way of thinking. In the first place, you must not let the brevity of the short story suggest to you that it is an easy thing to write. It is not: other things being equal, it is much harder than the novel, and is (incidentally) sold in a much more competitive market. Truman Capote calls it "the most difficult and disciplining form of prose writing extant"; in the difficulty of writing it well and in various other respects, it is more closely related to poetry than to the novel. "Maybe every novelist wants to write poetry first, finds he can't, and then tries the short story, which is the most demanding form after poetry. And, failing at that, only then does he take up novel-writing." Factually speaking, Faulkner was there over-stating his case: not every writer has that particular life-history. But the principle involved is a sound one. Look upon your first three novels, if you like, as a preliminary discipline, a preparation for the writing of your first short story: this might not be wise, but it would be more realistic than the converse proceeding.

In the second place, the novel does not differ from the short story only in the two matters of length and of relative difficulty. These are sharply different art-forms, and they call for very different gifts, very different habits of the mind. A writer can succeed beautifully in the one and fail grotesquely in the other. Some can succeed in both; but then, it's also possible to be at once a brilliant surgeon and a brilliant violinist. General brilliance can accomplish many things. But the aspiring novelist, uncertain still about his general brilliance, should not attempt too much at once; and he should not regard the short story as a training-ground for a task essentially similar but larger.

He must look elsewhere for the scales and exercises that will enable him to overcome that initial paralysis and inarticulacy.

In many cases at least, he will need to approach the problem at a more humdrum level. Let us assume that he has a reasonable command of language; let us assume also that he has a number of ideas buzzing around in his head more or less formlessly, visions of people and scenes and situations and relationships. His problem is to relate the two : he has to establish a working daily relationship between his mind's thinkings, casual but lively, and the physical act of writing fiction.

For most people, no such relationship is part of the mind's habit and furniture. The writing of narrative is an unfamiliar act : we simply don't do it. We write other things : letters to our friends, office memoranda, political commentaries, treatises on thermodynamics. And we all go in for narrative, of the oral or spoken kind : the conversation of some women appears to consist of little else. But until we sit down to write a novel or a short story, the writing of narrative is a thing that we don't do; and when we attempt it, we're a little at sea.

This fact may contribute to the difficulties of the aspiring novelist who can't get started on his novel. He sets out to do something both difficult and unfamiliar, and he sets out to do it (so to speak) in public : naturally enough he's overcome with stage-fright, and he dries up in terror, like an inexperienced actor.

Accept, then, the fact that unless you are one of the lucky ones, your first attempts at fiction-writing will not be publishable, or indeed satisfactory in any way : they will be comparable to the novice-fiddler's first squawks. You must be prepared to begin by writing rubbish. Don't be embarrassed : nobody else is going to see it and jeer, unless you are silly enough to leave it lying about the house. (This is one of the great charms of writing as a personal art and occupation. If you play, people will hear and wince; if you paint, they will peer over your shoulder and comment infuriatingly. But writing is done in a comforting solitude and secrecy.)

Set yourself a limited objective, therefore: for the time being, you must attempt merely to write fiction, without bothering in the least about the quality, or even the originality, of what you write. The physical action is the important thing. Some day, you are going to be a sound and even a brilliant novelist: meanwhile, and as a first step, you must simply try to become familiar with the act and routine of writing fiction.

Seen in these humble terms, the problem of breaking the log-jam ceases to be a literary problem: it becomes a psychological problem—a moral problem even, a matter of self-discipline. The only way to stop smoking is to stop smoking: the only way to get into the swimming bath on a cold day is to run straight from the changing-room into the deep end without stopping to ponder: the only way to become a writer is to write.

The practical conclusion is simple and obvious. You want to write a novel, and you find it hard to get started? Very well. You must take a most solemn vow, on the ashes of your fathers and the temples of your gods, that in the course of every week—or, better still, in the course of every day—you will defile and spoil with fictional writing (never mind its quality) no less than x sheets of perfectly good paper. This x need not be a very large number; but having made your vow, you must stick to it. Nothing else is going to save you from the ugly fate of those countless people—friends of yours, some of them—who really and seriously meant to become novelists one day, but never did.

And you can certainly do this, whether or not you have the novelist's gift. The essence of a vow lies in its literal fulfilment. You have promised to write fiction: you haven't promised that it will be good, and you haven't even promised that it will be original. At this stage, it will probably be quite without coherence and life and originality and every other kind of merit that might make it publishable. Never mind: you aren't aiming at publication—not yet. You are merely trying to establish a habitual familiarity with what is, for you, a new kind of activity; and you need to think of this not as wonderful creation but as a mere physical act—the act of pounding the keys or pushing the pen in such a manner that the result is, undoubtedly, 'fiction'—even though it may be fiction of rubbishy quality at first, even though it may not be wholly (or at all) your own.

Thus will you break the log-jam or melt the ice.

You can undertake this vow to write a specified quantity of fiction every day, and in good conscience: you need not fear that you will have to break it—most immorally—on the black days when your baby Muse deserts you. If the worst comes to the worst, if the paper obstinately stays blank, take down from the shelf same novel that you've enjoyed—somebody *else's* novel —and fulfil your day's quota by copying down a suitable amount of it, word by word.

This will not call for genius or inspiration. Do it in longhand, for choice: write slowly and meditatively, rolling each sentence around your tongue and your mind. It will be an exercise much less sterile and pointless than you might suppose: it will be a kind of dissection, it will offer you a close acquaintance with how fiction works, with its muscle and sinew, its structure and taste, such as you would never get from any casual reading of that same book, and certainly not from any work of criticism, any theoretical treatise on the novel.

Do this when all else fails. It will teach you a lot, it will form the habit, it will help you to grow out of your initial stage-fright, that initial shyness that may be compared with a painter's fear of the blank canvas. And it will at least enable you to keep your sacred and saving vow.

Upon this humdrum foundation, you can then start to build. Invent and imagine freely if you can; but if you can't, do it cautiously, by effecting small shy variations in what you copy. Doodle, improvise, play. You are going to be a powerful swimmer one day: meanwhile you must learn to feel at home in the water, you must overcome your natural fear of it, and this will mean a good deal of splashing and fooling around at the shallow end—even though such activities seem, in every immediate sense, to get you nowhere.

Only on your very blackest days will you be able to do nothing at all beyond a precise copying of somebody else's work. Don't underrate the value of this; but when possible, try to vary it— even in quite idiotic and irresponsible ways. Make arbitrary alterations to what you're copying, and see what effect they have. Reverse the sexes of the two people who are engaged in this conversation, and observe what kind of nonsense you get, and on what possible lines it might be converted back into some different kind of sense. Alter people's names : note how the potentiality and taste of a story is altered if Sally (who sounds blonde and cheerful) is transformed into Elizabeth (who sounds dark and reserved). Change the scene : take some passage that's set in a cathedral close at sunset, and re-write it (clumsily? all right, clumsily) against the background of a factory yard during a strike—or *vice versa*. Make the girl say Yes instead of No, and try to carry on from there. Strike out boldly, regardless of the consequences : vary, develop, omit, re-arrange, distort.

Play such games endlessly, in any silly way that happens to take your fancy; but always with close attention to what you're doing, to the consequences and effects that follow upon one operation or another of slicing and mixing and stirring. Don't try to memorise these—just let them sink into the mind. You aren't trying to work out a set of rules; you're only trying to get the feel of an unfamiliar activity.

Sooner or later, you will find that the proportion of mere copying is going down. There will be days upon which it dwindles to zero : you will find yourself inventing freely, if irresponsibly—your pen galloping ahead, your ideas tumbling over one another, your sketches and doodles being more and more the fruit of your own creative imagination, triggered off perhaps by a few words from somebody else, but then taking on a life of their own. You are moving freely and with increasing confidence—though, so far, unproductively—in the world of fiction-writing.

We have already seen Virginia Woolf in the throes of the total log-jam : let us now see her in the more constructive state that you have thus achieved. "Every morning I write a little sketch, to amuse myself. I am not saying . . . that these sketches have any relevance. I am not trying to tell a story. Yet perhaps it might be done in that way. A mind thinking."

Your mind thinks all the time : it always did, and on lines highly relevant to novel-writing. But its thoughts went fleeting away and were lost : you didn't have the general habit of catching them and making use of them. But now, between these casual thinkings and the act of writing fiction, you have managed to establish at least the beginnings of a habitual working relationship. Partially or completely, it may have been the absence of this that dried you up at the start.

Perhaps you are ready to make a start on that novel.

But the devil who inhabits the log-jam is a persistent devil, and you will never be wholly rid of him.

Having thus (and very laboriously) acquired a certain fluency in the act of writing fiction, and even in positive invention, you may still find it difficult to get the thing moving. Obstinately and (it seems) incurably, that first page stays blank.

At this stage, you may feel disposed to express your frustration in two distinct but related kinds of complaint. In the first place, you may say : "I want to write a novel, but I don't really know how. I must seek guidance; I need information, advice, help; I must master the precedents and the rules and the techniques." In the second place, you may say : "I'm sure I could write a novel : it's just that I can't work out a good plot. When I've done that, I'll be able to start."

In uttering each of these complaints, you will be expressing an idea that's almost a total delusion, but is widely cherished none the less. The first is the idea that there exists somewhere a general but definite technique of novel-writing, which needs to be learnt and understood and mastered in the first place, and then applied to the specific problems that arise in connection with some particular novel. And the second is the related idea that if there's a novel to be written, the first necessity is a well-contrived plot, summary, or synopsis.

Together, these two delusions amount to what might be called 'the technological fallacy'. We can easily see how it arises. We live in a technological society, and all around us we see clever men making wonderful things—cars, moon-rockets, surgical instruments, bridges, bombs. And we know very well how such things come into existence. First of all, the individual concerned —the engineer, the builder, the planner—must undergo a long course of training : he has to master the theory and practice of his job, as this has been worked out by his predecessors and established by their experience. Then, before any particular task is undertaken, the requirements need to be understood, the objectives need to be defined, the methods need to be chosen, a precise working plan must be carefully devised.

In general, that's how we do things. "First plan your work, then work your plan" : you'll never achieve anything (it is felt) unless you first arrive at a clear idea of whatever it is that you're trying to do. An engineer who has to build a bridge will survey the site, and the traffic and the loads and the winds and the local conditions generally; and to these data he will then apply the rules and principles that he learnt in the course of his professional training, as modified by the later experience of himself and others. Thus he will cause detailed plans to be made, with all materials and all methods carefully specified, so that the construction people will only have to do as they're told.

In matters more humble and domestic too, we assume that sound work depends upon this technological approach. In general, it does. A housewife who wants to make a cake will first decide what kind of cake will best please the family; then, from a cookery-book or her own experience, she will choose the ingredients and the methods that will bring about precisely the result foreseen and desired. She has to know what she's doing.

To most of us, this seems the only sensible way of going about any task; and hence, the aspiring novelist often tends to approach his particular task in the same way. He assumes that the process of writing a novel is analogous to the building of a bridge or the cooking of a cake; he casts about for rules and precedents and methods and techniques, and then he tries to begin by devising an outline plot or synopsis—this corresponding to the engineer's drawings or the housewife's recipe.

This is very natural: it reflects a deep-seated habit of the mind, usually relevant to many or most of our activities, clearly enshrined in our manner of talking. When we want to suggest hopeless incompetence and a certainty of failure, we say that the person concerned "doesn't know what he's doing".

But this manner of proceeding, most necessary if we are to have bridges and cakes, has only an occasional and limited kind of relevance to the novelist's task. Many novels or most are written by people who *didn't* know what they were doing—by people who could tell you little or nothing about the theory of the matter, and who began their work either with no idea at all, or else with a ludicrously vague idea, or even with a wildly erroneous idea, of what the end-product was going to be like and how it was going to work.

The fact is that the creative imagination functions in the dark of the mind, on lines that can be analysed afterwards but are not likely to be understood or controlled at the time, or planned or predicted in advance. The process is organic rather than technological: writing a novel is much more like having a baby than building a bridge.

Rules and precedents are therefore of doubtful value: the aspiring novelist doesn't need to have the critic's kind of cleverness, any more than the young mother needs to become an expert on embryology and genetics. Such things are interesting enough, but they don't help the painful task of bringing this particular baby or this particular book to birth. "All rules of construction," said D. H. Lawrence, "hold good only for novels that are copies of other novels." Two novels are not similar as two bridges or two cakes are similar: if they are, we suspect plagiarism and a lack of the new creativity that gives value to the exercise. Every bridge or every cake is a new solution to an old problem; but every novel raises its own problems, and it succeeds not because the author *knows*, but because the book itself *is*, the answer to those problems.

This last distinction may look like a quibble, but it is very crucial indeed. When engaged in his creative task, the novelist is indeed confronted by 'problems'. But there is a certain ambiguity in that word, and it needs careful handling. These problems are operational in nature, not theoretical or technological: abstract answers to them—prior to, and distinct from, the concrete existence of the finished book—are not merely elusive but inconceivable too.

There cannot be a positive technique of novel-writing: the only rule is: "Do it if you can get away with it." There can be a technique of bricklaying, because one brick resembles another; there can be a technique of surgery, because one human body is much like another and has the appendix in roughly the same place. "Let the writer take up surgery or bricklaying if he is interested in technique," says Faulkner; and "the young writer would be a fool to follow a theory. Teach yourself by your own mistakes; people learn only by error."

In writing a novel, therefore, you'll be working alone and in the dark, and at a task that you must not necessarily expect to understand. Your condition will be rather like that of a woman who has to produce her first baby alone and unaided in a remote and primitive place. There's nobody to help you, and there aren't any rules to follow. "Every attempt," says Eliot of a related art, "is a wholly new start, and a different kind of failure."

If this were not the case, if novel-writing were a skill handed down from master to pupil, developed progressively over the centuries, governed by rules and techniques that were understood with ever-increasing clarity and fullness, then the statistics of failure and success would have a different and a more encouraging pattern. When bricks are laid, the consequent wall tends—

in general—to stand up; when an appendix is removed, the patient tends—in general—to recover. But the writing of novels is not attended in any similar way by a general expectation of success. It's not a skill that our clever civilisation has mastered : it's more like a trick or a gamble that a few people inexplicably manage to bring off.

The publisher's reader passes his life in a landscape dominated by this sad fact.

The technological mistake is to be avoided in all its ramifications. You should not suppose, for example, that a degree in English Literature is going to be notably useful, amounting to something like a professional qualification. Studies of that kind may even hinder you, by overdeveloping the critical faculty at the expense of the creative faculty. (If you've decided to be a novelist one day, and in the meantime to go to a university, your best subject will probably be medicine.) And when you have written three novels successfully and had them published, you must not then look upon yourself as an established practitioner with an assured future. Your fourth novel may well be an inexplicable but total failure; and when the publisher turns it down, you may feel outraged at this gratuitous insult to your reputation and standing. Things of this kind happen frequently, causing great embarrassment all round.

In particular, do not envy the engineer his blueprint or the housewife her recipe. When you embark upon your first novel, you must not suppose that it's necessary—or even desirable—to work from a plot or synopsis fully worked out in advance.

All the evidence suggests that novels are seldom written in anything like that kind of way; or at least, that a totally different approach to the matter is thoroughly workable. When I sit down to write a novel," said Henry James, "I do not at all know, and I do not very much care, how it is to end." "I am a very irregular writer," confessed Samuel Richardson; "can form no plan; nor write after what I have preconceived." Stendhal

45

said that plotting or planning or designing in advance "freezes me stiff". Simenon writes his novels chapter by chapter, and to begin with he claims to "know nothing whatever about the events that will occur later. Otherwise it would not be interesting to me." "I don't believe the writer should know too much where he's going," said Thurber. "If he does, he runs into old man blueprint—old man propaganda."

Countless other novelists have written in similar terms; and the moral is that present vagueness about 'plot' gives you no kind of an excuse for not getting started. (The words just quoted from Thurber deserve particular attention, although he was never a novelist : the two nasty old men he mentions are to be avoided like the plague, unless you want to alienate the publisher's reader.)

But since people tend to be afraid of the dark and like to know where they're going, you may feel nervous about launching out into the unexplored depths of your novel without the reassuring support of some kind of plan or guide-book; and even though you admit that it's not necessary or even important, you may therefore *want* to do some degree of planning or plotting in advance.

But this may be less easy than you suppose. If you start from a blank sheet of paper, and attempt to devise what will seem—in the abstract—to be 'a good plot', you will probably find it rather hard to get a foothold. You will be dealing with abstractions and unknown quantities, attempting to finalise their pattern on a basis of insufficient knowledge : the enterprise will have an elusive and frustrating character.

The trouble is that 'a good plot' is not quite the same thing as 'the plot of a good novel'; and it's the latter that you will need. The quality of a novel is by no means a matter of soundness in the plot. "A very good or a very bad story can be written on the same plot," says Margaret Kennedy, "just as good and bad pictures may have the same composition line. Many stories, quite different in texture and implications, can be written on an identical plot."

46

The truth of this can easily be checked by experiment. Take some novel that you've enjoyed very deeply, and boil it down carefully into an outline summary or synopsis. You'll find that practically all the life has gone out of it; you'll be left with something devoid of all inherent attraction. It may remind you, distantly, of the actual book, but you could not bring it forward as proof that the book is a good one. It will be unlikely to seem either better or worse than a similar synopsis prepared from a comparable book that you haven't liked at all.

A novel most emphatically needs to have plot or structure, just as your true love needs to have bones. But you don't love her because of her splendid skeleton, and your acquaintance with her didn't begin with that aspect of her total reality—supportive and most important though it plainly is.

Design your book's skeleton in advance if you really want to. But your synopsis or scenario will not necessarily be helpful when you come to the actual writing. You may find, like Stendhal, that it freezes you stiff. You may—alternatively—find that while it does facilitate the production of a complete novel, it also guarantees that the story so written will be dead and mechanical. And as the actual writing develops, you will probably find it increasingly difficult to stick to the plan.

This is to be expected. As the book develops, page by page, you will begin to acquire a close and intimate understanding of your characters and the pattern of what's happening to them; by a process that is exploratory quite as much as creative, you will acquire the 'feel' of the novel, an instinct for what belongs in it and what doesn't, a close sympathetic involvement with its developing life. And this will probably be something quite different from the distant and theoretical knowledge you had when you drew up that synopsis.

Be prepared, therefore, for a conflict between the organically-developing story and the pre-ordained plan. You may have to choose between them. The danger is that your choice is likely to be biased in favour of the plan, especially if you're a beginner and under-confident. Once you've prepared your plan or synopsis, you're likely to fall somewhat in love with it. You know that it's only a working plan, an instrument, a means: still, it is—in its own way—a thing already accomplished, a concrete achievement as far as it goes, such as might (if you're foolish) be shown to friends. And it looks so fine and convincing and professional: you are anxious to live up to its promise, you don't want it to be wasted. Your actual novel, so far, is only a fumbling beginning: alongside that neatly-typed synopsis, it looks a poor and doubtful thing.

Thus tempted, you must always trust the live embryo rather than the dead skeleton. This may possibly have helped you to get started, and—an important point—it may have helped you to *believe* in your ability to write a novel. But it was drawn up when you didn't, in any real sense, *know* the novel that you were going to write; and in any case, it is only a synopsis. Don't take it too seriously at any stage. It is a thin faint thing: it must be. It can never stand in relation to your finished book as that engineer's drawings stand in relation to his finished bridge. The nature and purpose and life of the bridge can be wholly stated and defined in words and diagrams and figures, whereas a synopsis can never be more than a dim ghost of what a novel actually *is*. "This indeed is one of the significant facts about a true work of art," said Tolstoy, "that its content in its entirety can be expressed only by itself."

In the early stages at least, you will be well advised to look upon your task as an exploration of unknown territory rather than as the implementation of a plan. You are confronted with a question: "What *is* this novel that I propose to write?" And nothing short of an actual writing of the novel can constitute an answer.

There is a well-known story of a little girl who was told to be sure of her meaning before she spoke. Her answer was memorable: "How can I know what I think until I see what I say?"

Let that little girl be your patron saint: invoke her wisdom and power, against the stifling devil of the log-jam. There's a novel within you; and there is a real sense in which you can't write it until you know it. You can't come to know it by theoretical planning; a previously-devised plot is not a thing to be taken too seriously. You can only find out about your possible novel by writing it.

CHAPTER THREE

THROUGH DARKEST AFRICA

IN THE PREVIOUS chapter, a technique and an approach have been suggested that may be useful to the aspiring novelist who finds it hard to get started. Let him acquire a general fluency and confidence in the writing of narrative, if necessary, before he attempts the full creative task of writing an actual novel. And let him not be held back by any feeling of technical incompetence or by any vagueness about the ultimate plot and structure of his book.

With certain obstacles thus removed, he should be able to make some kind of a start. If necessary, let him write—as they say—by brute force and ignorance. Let him aim doggedly at the mere consumption of ink and paper, at the literal fulfilment of that vow; but in the continuity of a novel now, rather than (as before) in odd scraps. "I always figured the only way I could finish a book and get a plot was just to keep making it longer until something happens." So described—the words are Nelson Algren's—the task shouldn't seem too daunting.

But it's one thing to begin and another thing to continue; and the world is also full of people whose novels started confidently enough, but then ground to a standstill after one or two chapters had been drafted. In cupboards everywhere, in dusty files and in the bottom drawers of desks, there lie grubby old envelopes beyond all counting, each one containing the sad remains of an incipient novel that never reached full term.

In such a case, the possible novelist will usually be a little shamefaced about it. "I think I had something there; but I couldn't make anything of it, I couldn't go on." This will often be because he discovered, painfully, that the writing of a novel (or any sort of book) absorbs a great deal of time and energy —more than he thought, perhaps. His life was too full, he had other things to attend to: as soon as he found out that a novel can't be dashed off quickly and easily he dropped the idea; and who shall blame him?

Where his difficulty is of this kind, he cannot be helped— except, possibly, by the provision of time and money and solitude. A divorce might help him, or the loss of all his friends, or a long but mild illness, or a few months in some understanding kind of prison.

Often, however, the difficulty will take another form. He dropped the idea (he will tell you) because these first few chapters, laboriously written, filled him with an acute awareness that they weren't any good. It just didn't seem worth while to go on: he had quite lost his faith in the life and value of the end-product.

In this gloomy conclusion, he may be right. But it is a pity if he reaches such a seriously negative conclusion too soon, on the basis of insufficient evidence; and if this first draft of his first few chapters seems defective and thin, he should not take the fact too seriously. It proves very little. He may or may not be able to write a good novel: the question is still open, and it will remain open until a much later stage. Apparent or even manifest weakness in these opening fumbles is not evidence.

The beginning of any novel has to be good, of course; and it has to be good in two ways. In the first place, it has to function successfully as a mere beginning: that is, it must effectively catch the attention and interest of a possible reader. In the second place, it must be well related to what follows, it must constitute a sound launching of the whole.

But you must not necessarily expect to accomplish this twofold task successfully at the very earliest stage of your work, while the bulk of your novel still lies hidden in the dark of your sub-conscious. You may devise a wonderful beginning, and then find that it can't be related to what emerges subsequently; on the other hand, you may find it easiest to explore and exploit your potential book by way of a first-draft opening that will serve your purposes but not your reader's—an opening that will therefore need to be changed later on. In general, you must not expect to begin by staging a precise and telling introduction of something that you don't yet know. If you can do this, well and good; but you may not find it easy or even possible.

There must be patience and sustained faith: once again, submit to the drudgery of learning to walk, and don't expect to begin with a dramatic and arresting caper such as will give you immediate delight and bolster your confidence permanently. At this early stage, the drudgery of writing your novel will probably be the disheartening drudgery of writing a thoroughly weak beginning. Don't worry. It will be possible, and it will almost certainly be necessary, to go back and re-write those first chapters at a later stage, when the whole book is known to your conscious mind, and when you are therefore in a position to judge what kind of beginning will suit it best.

It may even be positively dangerous if you begin by writing a first few chapters that please you immensely and seem wholly and permanently satisfactory. In such a case, you may be reluctant to alter them, and even blind to their probable need of alteration; and this can lead to a particular pattern of failure, very familiar to the publisher's reader. A novel begins on lines that are sound and interesting, though less than brilliant: its general quality half-conceals the fact that in these earlier chapters there's an element of fumbling, of casting about. Then, about half-way through, it suddenly finds its feet, comes really alive, takes on a new quality of assurance and maybe of brilliance. It's easy to see what has happened. The author has written it on a straight-through once-only basis, and only at the mid-point—or thereabouts—did he really discover what it was that he wanted to do, and how it might be done. Having pressed on to the end, he should then have gone back and re-written the first part (if not the whole) in the light of this new understanding; and he might have done so, if only those first chapters had been more obviously a grope and fumble. But when he came to the end, his mind was full of a rosy glow, generated by the obvious success of the later chapters; bemused by this, he overlooked the relative uncertainty and weakness of the beginning. So he left it at that; and as it stands, his book is ruinously uneven, broken-backed, a sad disappointment when considered as a whole. A beginning more obviously and unforgettably imperfect might have led to a better end-product.

Success does not depend, therefore, upon your initial achievement of a good beginning; and you will be inviting a premature and erroneous kind of despair if you write two or three opening chapters and then pause to look back upon them in a spirit of gloomy appraisal. The time for despair comes later. For the time being, keep the critical and appraising part of your mind under strict control; give the creative mind its head, let it gallop forward freely and even wildly until the *whole* novel has come into some kind of existence. Then you may pause and consider the whole; and if you find it to be completely without any kind of embryonic life and strength, such as might be fostered and developed and brought out in one or two overall re-writings, you may throw it away and take up bee-keeping instead. But not till then: not on the evidence provided by two or three opening chapters.

The first sequence of your novel may therefore be written last of all, at least so far as their final version is concerned; and you are of course under no kind of obligation to draft the various parts of your book in the order of their eventual arrangement. "I write the big scenes first," said Joyce Cary; "that is, the scenes that carry the meaning of the book, the emotional experience . . . When I have the big scenes sketched I have to devise a plot into which they'll fit. Of course often they don't quite fit. Sometimes I have to throw them out. But they have defined my meaning, given form to the book. Lastly I work over the whole surface."

More usually, however, novels come into first existence in

something like their final sequence. Sometimes, when an author
is notably brilliant, the first draft can also be the last. Angus
Wilson has said that he first makes extensive preliminary notes
and then writes straight through, correcting—mainly by
deletion—as he goes along : when he reaches the end, his book
is ready for the printer. William Styron experiences "some
neurotic need to perfect each paragraph—each sentence, even—
as I go along"; and there is a great deal to be said for such a
practice, since even a temporary acquiescence in low standards
and bad work can do you harm.

But such methods of working can make difficulties if your
own talent is more limited, or imperfectly developed, or both.
A method slower, more laborious and repetitive, may then be
necessary; the element of exploration and experiment will be
greater, and if your work is to succeed in a competitive market,
it will probably need to be distilled and refined in a weary
succession of overall re-writings. James Thurber was not a
novelist, but he was a brilliant writer; and he has placed on
record the process by which his brilliance was achieved, in a
way that offers useful guidance and warning. "My wife took
a look at the first version of something I was doing not long
ago and said 'Goddamn it, Thurber, that's high-school stuff'. I
have to tell her to wait until the seventh draft, it'll work out
all right. I don't know why it should be so, but the first or
second draft of everything I write reads as if it was turned out
by a charwoman."

One can reasonably be appalled at the idea of a sevenfold
writing of even a short novel; and there may be comfort in the
fact that in the following passage, Moravia is referring to a
much smaller number of successive drafts. "Each book is worked
over several times. I like to compare my method with that of
painters centuries ago, proceeding, as it were, from layer to
layer. The first draft is quite crude, far from being perfect,
by no means finished; although even then, even at that point,
it has its final structure, the form is visible. After that I re-write

it as many times—apply as many 'layers'—as I feel to be necessary."

The moral of this is that you must be prepared for a long haul. Your novel will probably come into first existence in the form of an initial full-length draft; and in writing this, you will aim primarily at rough overall completeness. Crude preliminary achievement will get you further than any amount of sterile perfectionist dreaming. " 'Get black on white' used to be Maupassant's advice," says Frank O'Connor; "that's what I always do. I don't give a hoot what the writing's like, I write any sort of rubbish which will cover the main outlines of the story; then I can begin to see it." For the underconfident beginner, this will usually be a sound example to follow, though it comes from a writer of short stories rather than a novelist. Bash out some kind of a complete novel, and then make it into a good one by overall refinement and distillation. You very seldom meet a painter who starts at the top left-hand corner of his large canvas, working assiduously at some tiny patch about two inches square until he's brought it to final perfection, and then moving on to the next similar patch. Don't let yourself be crippled by a tactical mistake of this kind; don't suppose you have to write an excellent Chapter I, and then an excellent Chapter II, and so on. Let your whole picture be sketched out roughly to begin with, and then worked over—as a whole— until it's finished.

And the sad fact is that nothing short of a full first draft is at all likely to perform successfully the function of an initial sketch. Don't write unless you enjoy writing.

You have to begin somewhere. You won't need a 'plot', but you will need to have some kind of a starting-point. You already have the ideas, the raw materials of many novels; having lived for two or three decades at least in the world of people and happenings, you have a well-stored memory and a way of looking at life. All this may not be present to your conscious mind, but it's there, and it will come bubbling up to the surface as soon as you're fairly embarked upon the headlong chaotic business of writing your first draft. A few particular themes, a few characters, a few situations and actions are already festering and rumbling around inside your restless head, and with luck you'll have thought up a good title, which will be wonderfully useful in helping you to *believe* in the whole project. You are anxious to explore, to find out about the novel to which these things belong; and you will write this first draft in the mood of an explorer, hacking your way through dark jungles, not knowing what to expect but very impatient to find out.

Your actual starting-point will, in all probability, be something very small and particular. The pearl forms slowly and perfectly, but only around some small speck of irritant that has become uncomfortably lodged inside the oyster.

That word 'irritant' needs to be borne in mind when you cast about for a suitable point of departure, a pre-occupation that is going to govern and motivate the launching of your expedition. If the novel is to function successfully and powerfully, it needs to be built around something that engages your feelings, something that intrigues you, something that bothers you. If you feel restless, consider your restlessness: there may be something there that could constitute the heart of your novel. Remember the state that Dickens was in, when he was pregnant with *Dombey*: "Vague thought of a new book are rife within me just now; and I go wandering about at night . . . according to my usual propensity at such a time, seeking rest, and finding none." Make the most of any such feeling: somewhere inside it, you'll find your starting-point.

The thing that actually triggers you off—which may or may not be explicitly featured in your opening sequences—can take almost any form. It may be a scrap of overheard conversation, a happening witnessed, a person met, a news item, an object: anything, so long as it holds you and obsesses you. Henry James speaks of "the precious particle . . . the stray suggestion, the wandering word, the vague echo, at a touch of which the novelist's imagination winces as at the prick of some sharp point." Turgenev says: "All through my career as a writer, I have never taken *ideas* but always *characters* for my starting-point." "With me," says Faulkner, "a story usually begins with a single idea or memory or mental picture. The writing of the story is simply a matter of working up to that moment, to explain why it happened or what it caused to follow." George Eliot once found herself set in motion by a title: it came to her, out of the blue, while she was sunk in what she called "a dreamy doze". Hawthorne found himself struck most inwardly by the actual object that later provided him with a title—the scarlet letter, an 'A' cut from red cloth to be the adulteress's badge. Trollope's *Warden* was set in motion by a place—the cathedral close at Salisbury—and by certain wholly abstract reflections upon the right use of old endowments. Angus Wilson speaks of certain phrases or catchwords that were current in his family circle, and had acquired a richness of private meaning from repeated use over a period, and were therefore "a very powerful source of imagination".

Characters, titles, things, places, ideas, turns of phrase: all these can haunt the mind, setting it in a ferment, causing you to wander about at night, seeking rest and finding none. Cherish them. Considered intensely, explored in depth, related to your other experience, they can build up a certain painful pressure in your mind, until the day comes when you have to sit down and open the floodgates and pour forth that rambling incoherent first draft of a novel.

Upon this pain and pressure, the book's life will depend. Search for it, therefore; torment yourself. And as the pressure builds up, take care not to release it in some accidental and fruitless way. "Fiction-writing is a kind of magic," says Angus Wilson, "and I don't care to talk about a novel I'm doing because if I communicate the magic spell, even in an abbreviated form, it loses its force for me. And so many people have talked out to me books they would otherwise have written. Once you have talked, the act of communication has been made." It has been said that every writer is a frustrated talker; and in so far

57

as the nature and subject-matter of your novel is concerned, it's desirable to stay frustrated until a very late stage. Explain your embryonic novel to somebody else, and it's all too likely to die on you: there is abundant witness to this sad fact, and the moral is that no desire for help and advice, no impatience to sharpen your ideas on somebody else's mind or sort them out with the help of his wisdom, should tempt you into talking about your new novel. You must stay alone with it until the creative part of your task is completed.

Working in this solitude, starting from some speck of irritant that has lodged in your mind, and cherishing the psychological pressure that provides your motive power, you will therefore begin to write, getting black on white, "making it longer and longer until something happens".

But you cannot move off except in some particular direction; and while it is not in the least necessary to work out a detailed plot, you should have some kind of an idea about where you're going. "The novelist should, I think, always settle when he starts what is going to happen, what his major event is to be," says E. M. Forster. "He may alter this event as he approaches it, indeed he probably will, indeed he probably had better, or the novel becomes tied up and tight. But the sense of a solid mass ahead, a mountain round or over or through which . . . the story must somehow go, is most valuable and, for the novels I've tried to write, essential." Elizabeth Bowen puts it more simply: "Plot is the knowledge of destination."

In however confused and vague a fashion, you will probably need to know your destination before you begin to write. This knowledge, limited but intense, is one item in the check-list of equipment needed for a realistic beginning. Apart from this, you will need that starting-point or speck of irritant, and just a handful of specific material—a place, a movement of action, a very few people who will (at this stage) be strangers to you.

It will be no drawback if your destination is apprehended only dimly. "When I began *A Passage to India*," says Forster,

"I knew that something important happened in the Malabar Caves, and that it would have a central place in the novel— but I didn't know what it would be." A novelist commonly knows where he's going only in the limited sense in which an explorer knows where he's going. Think of some intrepid adventurer who may have set out, last century, to discover the source of the Nile. In a sense, his objective was clearly defined and known: 'the source of the Nile' is an expression with a perfectly straightforward meaning. But the reality corresponding to those words was not yet known: the expedition's purpose was a transformation of bare words into concrete experience.

And so he moved off, this explorer, into the dark and unpredictable jungle. He 'knew' his destination, and he moved off in what he hoped was roughly the right direction; but he didn't know what the source of the Nile was going to look like, and he didn't know exactly how he was going to get there, and he didn't know what dangers and discoveries and disappointments and excitements he would encounter in the course of the journey. The attraction and fun of the game lay precisely in all these uncertainties: without them, it would hardly have been an exploration, and it would not have attracted this particular hero. And in the event, the whole expedition may have proved fruitless and a failure; alternatively, it may have led to some rich and unexpected kind of discovery—one more interesting, perhaps, than the source of the Nile. But that declared purpose, or one like it, was necessary in order to provide the expedition with a dynamic, a motivation: lacking this, it would have ben a mere pointless wandering around.

When your novel is completed and published, it will hold your readers' attention partly by appealing to their curiosity: they will want to know what happened next, and how it all ended. But if that simple curiosity provided the chief part of their motivation in reading, you could gratify it at once; you could tell them in a few sentences how it all ended, and there'd be no need at all for this great thick book of yours to be either written or read. But the matter is less simple than that. They don't just want to be told about the source of the Nile, or shown aerial photographs of it: the expedition itself is the thing, with all its uncertainty, and the source of the Nile is only interesting as providing a destination or target, and therefore a pattern for the whole experience.

Your readers are a party of explorers, and you are their leader: it is their good fortune that a publisher intervenes, so that they aren't taken on expeditions that are entirely fruitless and dull. But they are fellow-explorers with yourself; they are not a party of tourists, being conducted around some well-mapped territory, and in this early and important stage of a novel's first drafting, you will know very little more about the country and its inhabitants than they do. "To an extent," says Elizabeth Bowen, "the novelist is in the same position as his reader. But his perceptions should always be just in advance."

Evelyn Waugh once spoke of the novelist's trade as being "dangerous", and he spoke from experience: there is indeed something sinister, as well as much that's mysterious and unpredictable, about the exploration that you propose to undertake. This is a journey into the dark of the mind, even if the resulting novel has a light and cheerful character: done sincerely, the exercise is likely to plough you up, disrupting the surface certainties, the habits of mind by which you live. And your will and consciousness will not be wholly in control: to some extent at least, you will be surrendering, opening yourself to the depths.

"What about the creative state?" asks Forster. "In it a man is taken out of himself. He lets down as it were a bucket into his subconscious, and draws up something that is normally beyond his reach. He mixes this thing with his normal experiences, and out of the mixture he makes a work of art." But Forster insists that "this stuff from the bucket, this subconscious stuff" is not "procurable on demand". It comes at odd times, not of the writer's choosing; and it will often come most fruitfully when he is—for most other purposes—not at his best.

"I know, for instance," says Eliot, "that some forms of ill health, debility or anaemia, may (if other circumstances are favourable) produce an efflux of poetry . . . the material has obviously been incubating within the poet. . . . What one writes in this way may succeed in standing the examination of a more normal state of mind." Ill health can indeed assist the creative process; so can exhaustion, or unhappiness, or (within limits) the release effected by drink or drugs.

There are some people to whom the process is an easy and natural thing : they are the fertile inventors, the vivid imaginers, the fluent and sometimes garrulous writers, and their problem is that of discipline and control. To the others, this advice may be given. They may not be able to summon up creativity at will, working hard and profitably with Forster's bucket from nine every morning until lunch-time; but let them at least refrain from obstructing it. The creative imagination breeds flowers that are usually small and shy to begin with : don't pull them up by the roots to see how they're getting on, don't trample them down with the heavy boots of critical appraisal. The time for that will come later : let them gather a little life and strength first.

In general, at this first and most creative stage of your work, don't *think* too fiercely and critically. A too-critical habit of the mind is a destructive thing : indulge it, and you may perhaps reach a state in which you can't begin to formulate any kind of sentence without at once thinking of seven utterly crushing reasons why it won't do. Give the inarticulate depths a chance. Too many novels come before the publisher's reader in a withered or stunted condition : they were pruned too soon and too disapprovingly, they weren't given the sun and the nourishment and the loving neglect that they needed in their infancy.

Up to a point, the creative imagination can be fostered, the subconscious mind and memory can be encouraged to yield up their secrets. The conditions mentioned by Eliot can be used fruitfully when they come upon you : it may not be a good idea to invite them, and it would certainly be rash to seek creativity in drink or drugs. But there are other techniques: most of them depend upon the effectiveness of random stimuli in liberating the subconscious mind from the custody in which it is normally retained.

It is a familiar experience: we all know that if we gaze at the clouds, or at the glowing coals of a fire, we start to see patterns and images that aren't there. The psychiatrist, anxious to peer into the horrid deeps of the mind, makes similar use of the Rorschach blots, asking us what we see in those wholly shapeless shapes. And there are on the market a number of 'plot-finding' devices which depend upon the same principle. Essentially, they work by putting before the user a random selection of ingredients, each of which might belong in some kind of story. The pattern-making instinct is strong, and confusion offers a natural challenge to the mind: confronted with these random particulars, one tries at once to relate them, to organise them, and in the attempt one draws upon one's subconscious, unbolting its doors and thus giving it a chance to work creatively.

For some people, such methods can have their value. Many of us would dry up completely if told to sit down at once and 'write a story': the generality of the command would paralyse the mind. But these same people would thaw out and start immediately to imagine and construct and create, if the same command were given in terms random but very specific—if they were told (for example) to write a story involving a sack of potatoes, a crippled night-watchman, a fast car, and the imminent danger of war.

It is interesting to note that Leonardo recommended, for the painter's benefit, a similar use of random stimuli for the purpose of triggering off the imagination. "You should look at certain walls stained with damp," he said, "or at stones of uneven colour. If you have to invent some backgrounds you will be able to see in these the likeness of divine landscapes, adorned with mountains, ruins, rocks, woods, great plains, hills and valleys in great variety; and then again you will see there battles and strange figures in violent action, expressions of faces and clothes and an infinity of things which you will be able to reduce to their complete and proper forms." Commenting upon this passage, Dr E. H. Gombrich says: "There are other passages, even more interesting, in which Leonardo discusses the power of 'confused shapes', such as clouds or muddy water, to rouse the mind to new inventions. He goes so far as to advise the artist to avoid the traditional method of meticulous drawing because a rapid and untidy sketch may in its turn suggest new possibilities to the artist."

The principle is an important one: can you honestly claim that you haven't already tried to marshal into some kind of story the four elements proposed in the last paragraph but one? For the novelist, any kind of experience can perform the function of those walls stained with damp, those stones of uneven colour —especially such experiences as are marked by blurring and confusion. By all means, therefore, make yourself an immense pack of little cards, and write upon each one some item that takes your fancy—'simple village maiden', 'villainous squire', 'foreclosure of mortgage', whatever you will. Then shuffle and deal them out before you, a few at a time, and see what you make of them. Such games can set the imagination racing. But you must not come to depend upon them; your creative imagination must develop its own muscles and learn to stand upon its own feet.

From Leonardo's remarks, it should be obvious why a chaotic first draft, full of loose ends and extraneous material, is much more useful to the aspiring novelist that a neat abstract synopsis.

The thing most needed, at this stage, is confidence. Press on through this dark jungle, always having your destination in mind, but never forgetting that success depends upon an interesting journey rather than an expeditious arrival. And the materials that will hold your party's fascinated attention are there already, in the dark of your own mind and memory. You don't have to create them: men can't create anything. It's a matter of selection. In the muddle and flux of what surrounds you, bubbling up from the released subconscious, you will recognise and choose those elements that are likely to forward the purposes of your novel; and in this recognition and choice, the novel itself will become known to your mind.

Even so, you won't—in any full sense—know what you're doing. Afterwards, when your book is published, people will come to you, full of praise and curiosity. "How do you *do* it?" they will ask; "where do you get your ideas, how did you think of the plot?" And you will answer, lamely but truthfully, that you simply don't know. This won't be believed; they'll assume that you have some wonderful trick or technique up your sleeve, and are too secretive or too shy to talk about it. The technological fallacy is widely cherished; novelists are expected and required to be *clever* people, consciously deploying elaborate skills. Forster complained of this. "People will not realise how little conscious one is of these things," he said, "how one flounders about. They want us to be so much better informed than we are."

The creative process is a mystery, not to be explained in terms of technique and cleverness. "No amount of delving into the autobiographical sources of novels," says Angus Wilson, "no analysing of the processes of creation, no revealing of the ambiguities of the writer's aims, can fully explain the making of a novel. Nor is an analysis of the craft of the novel a true statement of what the novelist believes that he is doing when he writes his book." "In all the time I have been writing novels," says Mauriac, "I have very seldom asked myself about the technique I was using . . . I write with complete *naïveté*, spontaneously. I've never had any preconceived notion of what I could or could not do."

Start, then, from a point that moves you; let your exploring be aimed—broadly—at some source of the Nile, some Cave of Malabar, so as to give it pattern and destination; remember that your novel *is* this journey, as well as being a thing that becomes known in the course of the journey. And having once started, do not look back in appraisal and doubt. Have faith: press on. The journey cannot be appraised until it's concluded.

Scarred, fly-pestered, exhausted, you will eventually arrive at your destination, though it may not be quite the destination that you originally had in mind. The explorer in you—that romantic and somewhat irresponsible figure—has done his task, and can now retire from the scene. A trail has been blazed, the country has been opened up, there are rough maps in existence, something is known about the natives' language and their curious ways. Now the developers and technicians can move in, with a view to the commercial exploitation of what you've discovered.

But these grim prosaic developers and technicians resemble that explorer in being (after all) only yourself; and there's a lot of work confronting them.

You have managed to make a start, and you have managed to continue to the end: in however imperfect a form, your novel now does actually exist. A third predicament remains, to be resolved or avoided. You don't want this book to be rejected by every publisher who sees it; and you must therefore develop and improve and refine it into a *good* novel—one that will please the publisher's reader and earn his recommendation, and so find its way through the slow machinery of publication and finally into the libraries and bookshops.

CHAPTER FOUR

TOIL AND TROUBLE

S O F A R , W E have been concerned with a purely creative kind of activity, with a process by which you can bring some kind of novel into some kind of existence. But this is not the whole story. "In a writer there must always be two people," says Tolstoy, "the writer and the critic." In the earlier stages of your work, you will probably have found it desirable to impose a certain discipline of repression and silence upon the critical part of your mind; now, as you try to develop this first draft into a publishable novel, it will need to be deployed with some severity. You are like the mother-bear of legend : your cub has been born, but quite formlessly, and it still needs to be licked into shape.

This severity may not come at all easily or congenially : you will need a certain detachment, a certain strength of character if you are to cast a really objective and critical eye upon your developing work. Mothers tend to be somewhat besotted about their children, blind to faults in them which are obvious to other people. You must overcome this tendency : before his work is completed and offered for publication, every writer must look upon it as sharply and savagely as possible, and from a number of angles. "To keep his errors down to a minimum," says W. H. Auden, "the internal Censor to whom a poet submits his work in progress should be a Censorate. It should include, for instance, a sensitive only child, a practical housewife, a logician, a monk, an irreverent buffoon and even, perhaps, hated by all the others and returning their dislike, a brutal, foul-mouthed drill-sergeant who considers all poetry rubbish." Recruit such a Censorate for yourself, maintain it inside your skull, and listen carefully to everything that these characters say at every stage of your revision.

With their help, and over a long period of hard work, this chaotic first draft of your novel will evolve into something that will earn a favourable response from the publisher's reader.

One word of caution must be uttered in advance. It has already been pointed out that readers' reports are, for the most part, negative : the experience here offered, for the benefit of the aspiring novelist, is chiefly an experience of failure. And the patterns of failure tend to recur : within limits, it is true to say that unsuccessful novels tend to fall into a relatively small number of familiar pitfalls. To a certain extent, therefore, this book must be a catalogue of faults and failings, a pathology of the novel, a list of the diseases and defects to which it is prone. In itself, this is no bad thing : it should be useful to the novelist if he is warned in advance about the points of danger, the black spots on the road that he proposes to travel, the faults and weaknesses that have most often proved fatal in the past and therefore need his particular care and attention.

But there are two drawbacks to this negative or pathological approach to the matter. In the first place, it may suggest that 'a good novel' is the same thing as 'a novel that's without specific definable faults and weaknesses'; it may foster a negative approach to the task of creation, and this can do nothing but harm. Positive faults do tell against a novel, of course; but they are very often curable, and they are seldom as disastrous as weakness or defect in a novel's life, its energy and point, its cutting edge. One often comes across a novel that is—in a sense—'faultless', but cannot be published even so. There's no life to it. Perhaps the life was squeezed out of it in the course of excessively severe revision; perhaps it never had any life worth mentioning. In such a case, there will be no straightforward answer to the author's outraged query "*Why* was my novel rejected? What was *wrong* with it?" There was nothing wrong with it : it was beyond criticism, just as a dead man's behaviour is beyond reproach.

There's no market for the novel that's "faultily faultless, icily regular, splendidly null". And so, when you are revising your first draft to make it acceptable for publication, you must look upon this task in positive terms. Try to see it as an enhancement of the book's life, and only secondarily as an elimination of its faults.

In the second place, it is a mistake to think too seriously in terms of objective faults and weaknesses, as though these were fixed and universal in character, and could condemn a book to rejection, just as a man's crimes might condemn him to prison or his sins to Hell. Books can indeed be imperfect and unsuccessful, but it would be very misleading to define their faults and failings in quasi-legal or quasi-moral terms: one can easily drift into a vague idea that certain set rules are in force, and that every author has the duty of obeying them, and that the publisher's reader will pounce mercilessly upon any infraction.

Such ideas are widely held by aspiring writers: they amount to another version of the technological fallacy. Things aren't at all like that in fact. The novelist's art is governed by no statute book, no Ten Commandments. There are no rules that he has to obey, and he is fully entitled to do exactly as he chooses—remembering always that if he fails to please, he only has himself to blame.

If, therefore, we assert that a certain novel has a particular named fault, we aren't blaming it for some breach of the statutes and commandments: we are only reporting our discovery that at this point—or in this respect—it fails to function successfully. Perhaps the author has attempted something beyond his powers; perhaps he has just failed to take the necessary trouble. Similar failures, recurring in a variety of novels, may well suggest a universal difficulty, and we may then be tempted to suppose that we have discovered a Rule, valid and binding for all men. "The novelist must not do so-and-so!" But there will always be some other writer who does what seems to be exactly the same thing, with total and effortless success.

68

Faults and blemishes are relative: what constitutes a fault in one writer will be no fault at all in another. "When we try to define the badness of a work," says C. S. Lewis, "we usually end by calling it bad on the strength of characteristics which we find also in good work . . . The novel before you is bad—a transparent compensatory fantasy projected by a poor, plain woman, erotically starving. Yes, but so is *Jane Eyre*. Another bad book is amorphous: but so is *Tristram Shandy*. An author betrays shocking indifference to all the great political, social, and intellectual upheavals of his age: like Jane Austen."

All talk of faults and weaknesses must therefore be interpreted with caution: these are merely the respects in which novels tend to fail when their authors are of less-than-perfect ability, the points at which an absence of genius will tend most easily to become manifest. At such points, you will do wisely to take a special degree of care. But you are fully entitled to do whatever you can succeed in doing: your novel will be judged upon the success that it actually achieves, not upon its conformity to any rules and precedents whatever.

There is a practical moral here. Be careful about following in the footsteps of the great masters: they can do things that you probably can't, they can ignore warning signs that you must take seriously. Above all, don't try to justify your failures by appealing to their precedent and authority. "Why do you say I was wrong to do so-and-so? Dostoievsky does it, and so does Graham Greene: it *must* be all right!" To any such complaint, the reply would be cruel and obvious.

With these cautions in mind, and with your internal Censorate criticising and objecting and sneering at every stage, you will embark upon your task of revising and re-writing and improving.

In order to assist this process and to improve the chances of a happy outcome, we shall—in the remaining chapters of this book—consider the various responses that your novel is likely to arouse in the publisher's reader. In the first instance, you're trying to please him: in giving shape and pattern and finality to this half-formed novel, you will do wisely to pay attention to his past experiences of failure and success, and even to his foibles and prejudices.

Not all of these will be, in the narrowest sense, literary. In its very first impact upon him, your novel will come before his weary eyes as a physical object, a thing that has to be handled and looked at. Ideally, its physical characteristics should not concern him: he has to pass judgment, not upon the actual typescript that you submit, but rather upon the nicely-produced book that it might become. He should not be irritated, therefore, by a typescript that's unsightly or grubby or unmanageable, and he should not be seduced by the skin-deep charms of perfect presentation. But he is only human, if that; he handles a great many typescripts, and suffers all the time from the various kinds of inconvenience that they can offer. Show him a little consideration. You cannot secure his love, with any certainty, by presenting your novel in a physically perfect form; but you can at least take care not to alienate his sympathies at the outset. You hardly want him to embark upon your first chapter in a mood of exasperation, hating the thing already because he can't handle it and read it in any comfort. It may be useful, therefore, if we begin our survey of the toil and trouble that now confronts you by considering your novel as a physical object that has to be generated by a physical process.

We speak of 'a writer'; and the word suggests in the first instance a man who—in Maurice Baring's words—has to "push a heavy pen over slippery paper, with feeble fingers and uncertain aim". But in these days, the word also suggests—perhaps more strongly—a man who pounds away at a portable typewriter.

Both skills are highly desirable, relevant in different ways to your task. Handwriting is a very distinctive thing, personal to yourself, closely tied in with the secret workings of your mind: for the initial and purely creative task of pouring forth your first draft, you will probably have found this the best medium. And it offers one particular advantage. A typewriter can only accept single sheets, which then have to be filed or stacked somehow; but if you use a pen or a pencil or a ballpoint, you can then write your first draft in a big thick fastbound notebook or two. And this may be a good thing. At that first stage, the flexibility of anything like a loose-leaf system would probably constitute a distraction : it would tempt you to look back and doubt and modify and revise and re-arrange, at a time when you should be pressing on. There is a lot to be said, initially, for that fast-bound notebook. If you want to make a small concession to your own underconfidence, you can write on the right-hand pages only, leaving the left-hand pages bare for subsequent notes and comments.

Now that the time has come for revision, however, flexibility is plainly a good thing. Some kind of loose-leaf file or binder is called for. And now that your task has become more critical and less creative than it was, the typewriter will impose upon your writing a detached and mechanical look that you may find helpful. "Much as I loathe the typewriter," said Auden, "I must admit that it is a help in self-criticism. Typescript is so impersonal and hideous to look at that, if I type out a poem, I immediately see defects which I missed when I looked through it in manuscript." Print is even more detached and impersonal, of course : if you have never yet been published, you will be astonished to see how strange and alien your own writing appears when printed. Typescript, coming between handwriting and print, may help to save you from the distress of recognising defects, and desiring to correct them, when it's too late.

At some stage before your novel is finished and ready for its final fair-copy typing, you should therefore cause it to exist in the form of an overall rough typescript, widely spaced so as to facilitate corrections. Let this be chopped and changed and possibly re-typed until you are finally and completely satisfied with the result. Unless you are very confident and assured, don't try to combine the final typing with a final revision. Last-minute inspirations are dangerous. Whether it's done by yourself or by an agency, let the final typing be a matter of straight literal copying.

This is, perhaps, a theoretically ideal method of working: longhand in a fast-bound notebook at your first-draft stage; then a series of progressively-improved typescript versions, messed around and modified until the whole book comes exactly right; and finally a fair copy. But people are individuals; and since writing is not a wholly rational activity, it cannot always be governed by nicely rational considerations. You will have to evolve your own method of working. Some novelists can only think at the typewriter; others are distracted by its clatter, and prefer the silent pen; some find it possible to mutter their first thoughts into a tape-recorder, and then have the result typed out for revision. And there are many who find themselves irrationally and even superstitiously addicted to certain particular methods and materials and circumstances. You must not be surprised or worried if you find yourself wholly dependent upon some special kind of paper, unable to write a word upon any other kind: an unfamiliar typewriter or the wrong make of ballpoint can paralyse you in the same way. If so, you are in good company: many great novelists have had similar quirks of the mind and habit. The thing to do is to cast about and experiment until you've discovered what your own personal lunacies are, and then—in general—to indulge them.

This applies to the circumstances as well as to the methods and materials of writing. One novelist works in a style that would be an office-manager's delight: he has his quiet study, his regular hours, his colour-coded files, his progress-charts, his fastidious precision of method at every point. Another can only think and work in an atmosphere of turmoil: in some crowded and jostling bar, he'll be scribbling away on the back of an envelope, and his desk (if he has one) will be a hideous mess of inky confusion. Not everybody works at his best when circumstances appear to be perfect. The rural serenity of that country cottage may dry you up completely: your novel may need to be written in an airport lounge, or perhaps in the kitchen at home, with the children tugging at your skirts, so that there's jam on the finished article. Faulkner was once offered the job of landlord in a brothel, and gave various reasons for regarding this as an absolutely ideal environment for the literary man. Some write best in the early morning, some at dead of night; some when modestly drunk, some when infamously sober. Many like to have some totem or fetish before them on the desk or table, and are lost and miserable without it.

Empirically, you must discover the circumstances that make writing easiest and most fruitful for you. But beware of self-deception. If you find that your productivity depends upon materials and circumstances that are only seldom likely to be available, distrust the fact: semi-consciously, you may be cooking up reasons for not writing at all. In particular, you must try not to be too much at the mercy of your own moods: don't shelve the job until your life and mind have been sorted out completely, or you'll shelve it for ever. "If writers had to wait until their precious psyches were completely serene," says William Styron, "there wouldn't be much writing done." There is ample reason for distrusting your own moods. Most writers will tell you that their best work has been done when they felt wretchedly flat and uncreative; and conversely, that the passages that felt most deeply inspired, and were written most easily in a mood of high euphoric confidence, often turned out to be rubbish. Feelings, at the time, don't signify very much.

"Hold-fast is the only dog": stubborn application is prominent among the factors that are going to make your novel publishable.

The laboriousness of all this has already been stressed; and you should be warned also that success may depend—in your own particular case—upon very intensive concentration over a relatively short period. You may only be able to write a novel at all if you can drop everything else until it's finished. This is a matter of temperament. Some novelists can write and revise a book over a period of years, working in slow fragmentary fashion, taking it up and then laying it aside again, perhaps working concurrently upon two books or more. If your creativity functions in this way, it will be easier for you to combine the novelist's trade with a variety of other tasks and preoccupations. But you may find that your novel goes off the boil and dies on your hands unless you can produce it in one intense period of single-minded effort. Its genesis depends upon a certain steam-pressure in the mind, and this is easily dissipated unless it is kept up by constant attention. If you once lay the book aside and let it drop out of your mind, you may find it almost impossible to pick up the threads again. The very idea of returning to it will fill you with horror and revulsion. Charles Morgan once compared the experience of resuming work on unfinished novel with the experience of putting on dirty clothes after a bath: Simenon reports that if illness interrupts his writing, the work done so far is wasted and has to be thrown away.

This is something like a general experience, though there are many exceptions. Having once begun, you should press on; and if your writing has to be done in spare time and odd moments, you are going to need a great deal of discipline and dedication.

At the last stage but one, you will therefore find yourself in possession of an object that seems to you quite perfect in every literary way, though it is still a horrible mess to look at. Basically, it's a wide-spaced typescript; but it's cluttered all over with corrections and alterations in smudgy ballpoint, there are balloons and arrows, odd bits are taped or stapled on at angles, the pages have been radically re-arranged and re-numbered half-a-dozen times. It would be an act of heartless cruelty, and of gross imprudence too, if you were to submit the thing in this disgusting form.

You will therefore cause it to be re-typed—by your own hands if they are clever at the keyboard, or else by some friend or some professional. You know very well that few publishers will consider a hand-written offering.

The thing to remember, at this stage, is that your typescript is going to be read by many people and in various circumstances. This, at least, is what you hope for. Many novels are of course rejected—and *rightly* rejected—after a single cursory examination by one person. But your novel is going to be something of a success, and it will therefore pass through a good many hands. It will probably be skimmed through, in the first instance, by some retained reader of relatively junior status: this character will not have to decide whether it's fit for publication, but only whether it's fit for serious consideration. Having survived this first test, it will then be passed to some senior reader of immense prestige and authority, such as myself; and then, perhaps to another. After that—if all goes well—it will be taken home, at successive week-ends, by one or two editors of the publishing firm that you've approached, and then perhaps by one or two directors. Later on, when the great decision has been reached, it will be handed over to certain slaves for copy-preparation—a detailed polishing in such respects as punctuation and the use of capitals, a removal of countless blemishes and inconsistencies that you hadn't noticed. It may go through another similar treatment when it gets into the printer's hands; and then it will have to be used by the compositor who sets the type, and then by the printer's proof-readers, and then by yourself when you're correcting the galley-proofs, and then again when the page-proofs come in. Books are bred by a complex process.

Remember, also, that your typescript will have been through some further preliminary handlings if you employ an agent; and be prepared for the possibility that it may only be accepted by the seventh publisher who sees it, and that the earlier stages of this complex process may be repeated six times, or even more.

The world already contains quite enough eye-strain and bad temper: for pity's sake, don't add to it gratuitously. Let your book be submitted in a form that can be easily and comfortably read by perhaps fifty different people, one after another, without coming to pieces in the process.

A typewriter-ribbon can be bought for the cost of a double

whisky or a very modest lunch; and with an old toothbrush and a drop of spirit, it's very easy to keep the machine clean and the output readable. There's no excuse for the typescript that's hard to read, for the clogged characters and the pale faint impression: don't be guilty of this all-too-common rudeness. Then, let the paper be of adequate substance. Very thin paper will certainly save you or your agent a little money when your typescript has to be mailed across the wide Atlantic; but it will irritate the publisher's reader—and everybody else—if it's difficult to read because every page is haunted by the ghost of the following page and also by the fainter ghost of the page after that. Let the stuff be sufficiently opaque : try it out before you buy it.

Let it also be of manageable size. Of these forty or fifty people who are going to read your typescript, some will be working in the office and at a nice spacious desk. But others will take it home and read it in the tired evening, slumped back into an armchair; if the thing can't be handled comfortably on the reader's knee, it will inflame his always uncertain temper. Avoid therefore, the size that's called 'foolscap' in England and 'legal' in America : stick to quarto, of the smaller British or the larger American variety. Allow reasonable margins : don't type right down to the very bottom of the page. And if your typescript is single-spaced, you will richly deserve the hatred that you incur. Double-spacing—or at least, the one-and-a-half spacing that can be done on most typewriters—is an absolute necessity.

Remember that your name and address will be typed on your title-page and will thus become known to the publisher's reader. Be warned. If your novel is single-spaced and typed invisibly and cloggily right up to the edges of your uncomfortably large and ridiculously thin paper, I shall still give it the report that it deserves on strictly literary grounds. But I shall also come around to your house one evening and beat you silly with a great thick cudgel.

Then, let your pages be numbered. At some stage in their complex history, they're very likely to slither off somebody's knee and get chewed a little by his excitable dog: don't make the task of re-arranging them an impossible one. And if your novel is submitted with its seven hundred pages neither numbered nor fastened together, as novels are submitted from time to time, the fact will carry a strong and perhaps indelible suggestion that you're an awful fool. Don't let this be thought too early : give the novel a chance.

There's nothing wrong with submitting your novel in the form of single sheets, a stack of typescript, not bound in any way, so long as these single sheets are numbered. The main thing is to make sure that it's soundly packeted or boxed. In these over-packaged days, your typing paper probably came in a nice neat box : you can use that same box for the finished article, and only a long novel will be too fat to squeeze into a ream-sized package. The danger is, of course, that sheets can get disordered or even lost.

The best answer is probably to staple them together in small batches of about fifteen or twenty pages. Don't staple them all the way down the left-hand edge : if you do, they will pucker tiresomely when they're folded back. Use a single staple, put diagonally across the top left-hand corner; and don't let any batch include more pages than one staple can bite together securely. This is a very sound arrangement. The pages can be turned back easily, none of them gets lost, there's no heavy burden upon the reader's arthritic knee. If the batches coincide with chapters, or with sections of chapters, that's excellent : if not, there's no need to worry. The successive batches can be stowed for postage inside a pocket-file or wallet, or even a strong envelope.

The publisher's reader will love you at once if your novel comes in this easily-managed form. But he will hate you passionately if it comes in certain other all-too-popular forms. One of the worst consists of thin sheets that are punched and then tied together, inside a flimsy cover, with a kind of orange bootlace. If you try to read this typescript like a book, you can't open it flat : you have to guess at the first two words of every line. If you try to peer into the middle, there's a tearing sound. So you untie the bootlace; but then the whole thing disintegrates, the holes tear, pages fall out : you find yourself trying furiously to re-assemble it at three o'clock in the morning, pushing that wretched bootlace through holes that aren't ever lined up properly, hating the man who invented literature.

Things can be even worse if there are brass fasteners instead of that bootlace. These have razor-like edges, and if they're at all loose they tear the paper disastrously. Often they are thrust through the typescript from the front and opened out at the back : it's dangerous then to rest the thing on your knees, since the slightest movement of those spikes will plough a bloody furrow down your thigh. Sometimes, instead of brass fasteners and bootlaces, there's a terribly intricate little clip, involving bits of bent tin and several springs and a long lever that's supposed to be held down under a little hook; sometimes there are spiral metallic worms and black plastic slides; sometimes there are sharp tongues that are meant to be retained under little sliding bits of tin. *All of these devices invariably go wrong.*

Only a shade less horrible is the typescript that comes in one of those spring-back files, made like a loose-leaf stamp album. For whatever reason, this one tends to be typed on unnecessarily thin paper; even so, there's always more of it than the file really wants to hold. About a third of it is loose, and cascades to the floor as soon as you open the parcel. Cursing obscenely, you sort it out and force it back into the file, nipping your finger in the process and raising a nasty blood-blister; then you try to read it, but the central spring is so tremendously powerful that you have to hold it open with the full muscular force of both arms. Before long you're running with sweat.

The fact is that most kinds of files are designed for storage : they're meant to hold such papers as will only need to be referred to occasionally, and can be extracted as necessary for prolonged individual scrutiny. They aren't really meant for continuous reading.

Don't use any kind of file unless you're quite sure that it *can* be read in comfort; in particular, it must be easy to turn the pages over repeatedly without tearing them out. Distrust everything that involves the punching of holes and the insertion of metal or string; and whatever file you use, don't overload it. Use several if necessary. But for choice, avoid every kind of file and fastener. Submit loose sheets, carefully numbered and boxed, or sheets stapled together in small batches on the lines already indicated.

From time to time, one comes across an author who has decided to by-pass all these problems and give the publisher's reader a real treat. His typescript arrives in book form, properly bound, and it's a joy to behold. He has chosen a pure hand-made rag paper of dazzling whiteness, and he's used one of those fancy typewriters that have proportionate spacing and a carbon-paper ribbon, so that the novel appears to have been printed already, and in a luxury format. Each page has been laid out beautifully; and the whole thing has been bound up in purple puma-skin and the heaviest of boards, with headbands and gilt edges and marbled endpapers and a lovely broad silk marker. The title and the proud father's name are tooled in gold upon the spine. You gasp with admiration when you see this miracle of craftsmanship.

But efforts of this kind are always wasted, and for two reasons. In the first place, compositors always prefer to work from single sheets; and if this novel were to be accepted, it would have to be ripped to shreds almost at once. The thought is enough to break anyone's heart. But it won't be accepted. By every literary standard and for every practical purpose of publishing, *books submitted in this kind of format are always worthless.* No body knows why this should be so, but it is so: it amounts to a law of nature, mysterious but absolute. Don't suppose that your novel will be an exception.

While taking care not to incommode and annoy the publisher's reader by the physical presentation of your novel, you should not try to charm him : your typescript should not clamour for attention and admiration. Good manners are unobtrusive: a workmanlike approach inspires confidence.

The ideal situation is one in which there's nothing whatever to distract him from purely literary considerations when—upon some fateful day—he takes up your novel, settles back in his chair, sighs deeply, and turns to Page One.

CHAPTER FIVE

TELL ME THE OLD, OLD STORY

IT IS YOUR desire that this novel should arouse a powerful and positive response in everybody who sits down to read it; and initially, in the publisher's reader.

Perhaps the first requirement is that it should, in some way, live up to the implications of that word 'novel'. It has to be new, it has to be original; otherwise it may arouse a response that's powerful indeed but not at all positive. In the vocabulary of the publisher's reader, there are few words dirtier than 'stale', 'second-hand', and 'derivative'; and things are going to be difficult if your first thirty pages provoke an agonised cry of "Oh God, not this old routine *again*!"

The need and even the possibility of originality can, however, be exaggerated. There are some novelists—usually feminine—who spend profitable lifetimes in writing the same book over and over again; and there are certain types of novel to which people turn for the re-enactment of a soothing and familiar pattern. Some light romances, some classical detective stories, some thrillers, some Westerns succeed by being exactly what the reader is used to. If you're writing for this kind of market, you'll only upset people if you start being clever and different. But even here, you mustn't copy: your originality will operate in a narrow and prescribed field, within strict conventions, but it still needs to be there.

Whatever kind of novel you produce, the most important part of its originality will arise from the fact that you, its writer, are quite unique. Your genetic make-up, your environment, your past, your experience, your psychology, your responses—all these things are as distinctive and unique to yourself as your fingerprints are; and so, if your novel comes from the authentic 'you', it will have the only kind of originality that really matters, and quite possibly the only kind of workable originality that's available.

This is not always recognised; and a great many novels fail because their authors strove in too agonised a fashion after other kinds of originality—usually in respect of plot or method or both. Such strivings are commonly a waste of energy, as C. S. Lewis points out: "The pother about originality all comes from the people who have nothing to say: if they had, they'd be original without noticing it." The possibilities of plot are limited; they have been analysed theoretically from time to time, and it has often been concluded that there are only six basically different stories—or fifteen, or twenty-two—so that we'll all have to ring the changes on these for ever. There is probably something in this. The publisher's reader comes across many delights and horrors, but only very seldom does he come across the novel that owes its success to radical and striking originality of plot. In general, this isn't a thing that you need to bother about. Shakespeare never bothered about it.

Originality of method is something else that you can easily take too seriously: many a perfectly sound novel has been ruined by the author's anxiety to stage it in some surprising and gimmicky fashion that hasn't been tried before.

One can understand the temptation. In these happy days, our minds work naturally on lines that are evolutionary and developmental; we like to think of ourselves as engaged always in technical elaboration and improvement, doing things that our fathers couldn't have understood, advancing ever onward towards greater and more complex achievements. Our scientific and technological achievements do indeed have this pattern, and their prestige is high: instinctively, therefore, we want our other activities—our arts, even our theology—to follow that same pattern. Hence, we're predisposed to favour the novel that's technically new, the 'experimental' novel; and all the more so, since this is the one that the critics will find significant. To them, a novel tends to be interesting and important in so far as it invites or compels their kind of interpretation and commentary : if there aren't clever things to be said about it, they are more likely to pass it by, however pleasing and satisfactory it may be in other respects. And the critics are a powerful priesthood.

The aspiring novelist, therefore, will often feel a strong compulsion to present his novel in some fashion that's odd and complex and difficult and *avant-garde* : under the influence of this compulsion, he would think you absurdly simple if you suggested that it was his prime task to please people by telling a good story well. He sees himself as having a loftier destiny, more arduous for all concerned.

A few people in each generation can be regarded, perhaps, as having that loftier destiny in fact; and they will naturally come in for an exceptional degree of critical attention. The danger arises if they are regarded as setting a trend which other novelists are then obliged to follow, under penalty of seeming dated. Countless novelists torment their work to death, quite gratuitously, because of their anxiety to be advanced and sophisticated and contemporary. It's a great waste.

In nine cases out of ten, the aspiring novelist should look upon his craft in eternal rather than in evolutionary terms. Beneath whatever varnish of sophistication, it still retains an archaic and even timeless character : it is an art that began with language and is as old as the human race. "History develops, art stands still," says Forster; and he suggests that we should exorcise the "demon of chronology" and look upon all novelists—ancient and modern—as though they were all writing side by side and simultaneously in some great big circular room.

Unless you are writing a historical novel or some vision of a remote planet or a possible future, you will presumably stage your story in a world or a time that you yourself have experienced; and in this sense your novel will be 'contemporary', drawing upon present-day life for its subject-matter. But in all other senses, there is great danger in the idea, the cult of contemporaneity. The fashion of the moment has its value : pioneers and innovators are praiseworthy and useful, recent ones included. But they should be regarded as extending and broadening the technical resources that are available to us, not as setting a trend that has to be followed in narrow strict obedience.

Some people talk as though the invention of the atomic bomb meant that the bow-and-arrow ceased in 1945 to be a lethal weapon, which is not the case; and some people are under very similar illusions about the arts. "After Proust," says Françoise Sagan, "there are certain things that simply cannot be done again." This is mere provincial snobbery, comparable to that of an old-style hostess who might say "There's absolutely *nobody* in town!"—meaning that the thirty-two members of her own small set had left for the country.

Use whatever resources seem to be available and relevant to your purpose of the moment; but don't let your concept of what the novelist can do and can't do be limited by any vogue or fashion of the moment. "Nice customs curtsey to great kings." Don't take the idea of the 'experimental' novel too seriously : when you come to think of it, there's nothing at all in the arts that corresponds at all closely to the part played by experiment in the natural sciences. That is a deceptive phrase. Don't feel, therefore, that you're obliged to be a technical innovator; don't worry about originality of method. If you feel disposed to use some method that's never been done before, bear in mind the possibility that there may be very good reasons for its neglect in the past. It may be impossible; it may be quite possible but not worth doing.

The novelist needs to keep his feet on the prehistoric ground. In so far as his art is subject at all to evolution and development and progress, it has quite probably reached the limits by now and explored the whole of the available territory. As a technician, the novelist is very seldom engaged in anything like a pioneering venture, an exciting set of experiments, a knowledge-explosion : essentially, he is still the old story-teller by the camp-fire, or—as Margaret Kennedy puts it—"the voice that told about The Three Bears at bedtime." Your work must have its life-line cherished and kept intact : it must never wander too far away from being something that might begin "Once upon a time . . ." and end ". . . and they all lived happily ever after."

Clever tricks, unless they're thoroughly well justified and very expertly performed, are likely to fill the publisher's reader with gloom and weariness.

Unless you are one of a small minority, therefore, you should allow your novel's originality to depend upon its emergence from a 'you' that's authentic and unique. The difficulty is that this authentic 'you' may be somewhat hard to discover. We all play-act, posture, and generate fictitious personalities, deceiving ourselves or other people or both : any novel that emerges from one of these false stage-selves is likely to be fictitious in quite the wrong sense. There is still great practical value in the old advice "Know thyself".

Let your novel be authentically your own : don't write up or down. If you are by nature a moralist or a social philosopher, the fact can be allowed to colour your writing, giving it a serious kind of importance; if you are by nature an amusing and frivolous fellow, then amuse your readers and don't be ashamed of it. People should wear clothes that fit them.

The publisher's reader often comes across a novel that has to be rejected because the author, in writing it, was acting in some serious degree out of character : he was wearing the wrong clothes. This is sometimes a matter of an awkward bending down, to something conceived as a lower level : an author essentially serious-minded makes elephantine attempts to be lowbrow and light and frivolous, and the result can be an embarrassing spectacle, like that of the vicar's wife jiving. But the opposite case is the more usual. One comes across somebody who might have been perfectly satisfactory as a straightforward entertainer, but who none the less feels a kind of compulsion to be immensely serious and profound and significant. And this too can be an embarrassing spectacle.

It is easy to see why this particular mistake should be made so often. Since the nineteenth century, the art of prose fiction has taken on a kind of dignity that it didn't have before. "The man or woman who publishes writings inevitably assumes the office of teacher or influencer of the public mind." These are the words of George Eliot, and Trollope wrote in similar terms : "I have ever thought of myself as a preacher of sermons, and my pulpit as one which I could make both salutary and agreeable to my audience." These are very Victorian sentiments, and their pattern is repeated right up to the present time. "The fiction-reading public is no longer scolded for a frivolous waste of time," reports Margaret Kennedy. "On the contrary it is, week in and week out, urged to accept Reproofs, note Salutary Reminders, hearken to Timely Warnings, and swallow Cathartics ... No reviewer likes to praise a novelist just now, without including some certificate for his civic conscience." This was written some years ago, and things have changed a little, but there's still a dreary amount of truth in it.

The novel is, in a sense, always on the defensive. In its very early days, the story-teller's art was associated—very reasonably —with pornography; and until that nineteenth-century seriousness set in, it was widely looked upon with a certain disapproval, as a thing frivolous at the best and often tending to corrupt. "A writer of novels and a dramatic poet is a poisoner, not of the bodies but of the souls of the faithful, and he should regard himself as guilty of an infinite number of spiritual homicides" : St.-Cyran was expressing here a Jansenistic view and an extreme one, but it was not only strict Christian moralists who thought on these lines. Much more widely, novels and plays were regarded as the exact opposites of any serious or useful reading— a fact amusingly illustrated by Sheridan. "Quick, quick—Fling *Peregrine Pickle* under the toilet—throw *Roderick Random* into the closet—put *The Innocent Adultery* into *The Whole Duty of Man*—cram *Ovid* behind the bolster—there—put *The Man of Feeling* into your pocket—so, so—now lay Mrs Chapone in sight, and leave Fordyce's *Sermons* open on the table." George Eliot herself would not have liked the novelist's art to be defined initially in terms of pleasing : the writer who merely 'gives the public what it wants' is (she says) to be compared with the proprietor of a gin-palace—a serious accusation, gin-palaces being what they then were.

Alongside the other and more optimistic view of the matter, this attitude still survives. With part of our minds at least, we still contrast novel-reading with 'serious' reading : the library will give you extra tickets for the one but not for the other, 'non-fiction' being more meritorious. Some people look vaguely guilty and embarrassed if you catch them reading a novel : in extenuation, they plead that it's a serious and important novel, a vital and significant contribution to something or other. Others feel that it's somehow wrong, the mark of a decadent and irresponsible character, to read novels *in the morning*, even when you're on holiday : you should save them for the late tired evening, or for long journeys, or for reading yourself to sleep.

As it exists in many people's minds, therefore, the novel is a thing not quite sure of itself, needing justification, having to stand on its dignity. Fortified by that distrust of mere pleasure that still marks the post-Puritanical English mind, this mood generates a certain anxiety that the novel should be a very solid and serious thing; and it often tends to be written in rather that spirit, by people who aren't in themselves very serious or stodgy at all. It is as though they thought : "I'm not just telling bedtime stories to the children, not now : I'm engaged in writing a Contemporary Novel. And the Novel is Literature; and Literature is a very serious grown-up matter. So at all costs I must be weighty and significant." If they have talents that are appropriate to this specific kind of purpose, there's no harm done. But if they haven't, there's spoiling and waste.

At a time when we all tend to take culture and the arts a shade too pompously, there's something to be said for cutting 'The Novel' down to size. It isn't philosophy, it isn't moral theology, it isn't social and political analysis : neither as often nor as easily as some people suppose can it contribute usefully to the questions studied by those disciplines. Sometimes it can : more often it will not, and will die in the attempt if it tries too hard.

Write, by all means, at the height of your ability. The attempt to talk down to your readership usually fails. One sometimes meets a clever person who proposes to make some easy money by putting his tongue in his cheek and writing trash for the pulp magazines; but the attempt seldom succeeds, since even this kind of literary success depends upon sincerity and striving. Dorothy Parker stressed the point. "Garbage though they turn out, Hollywood writers aren't writing down. That *is* their best." Write something less than your best, and it won't be printed—not even by a publisher who seems (by your fastidious standards) to be splendidly undemanding. You can't write with your tongue in your cheek. But it's equally fatal to talk *up* to your readership, assuming a false solemnity of purpose that doesn't belong. Be yourself : wear your own clothes.

In the last resort, the whole business of novel-writing and novel-reading does have a certain frivolity, an unimportance : as indeed does poetry. These things don't fill bellies or heal wounds or save souls. "The condition of mankind," says Auden, "is, and always has been, so miserable and depraved that, if anyone were to say to the poet : 'For God's sake stop singing and do something useful like putting on the kettle or fetching bandages,' what just reason could he give for refusing? But nobody says this."

Nobody will say it; and you needn't feel under any obligation to sing about the kettle and the bandages. Don't worry : just seek to please. This won't be wicked social irresponsibility on your part. By almost any reckoning, people need to be pleased—and distracted, and amused, and comforted, and illuminated inwardly, and warmed, and generally made happy—far more deeply than they need to have more Significance thundered at them.

Authentically yours, existing at your own natural level, and having therefore the basic and necessary kind of originality, your novel may still resemble a lot of other novels rather too closely.

It may still cause the publisher's reader to cry out in distress, as at an old routine that has been performed once too often.

Here again, there's a particular danger for the novelist who's over-anxious about contemporaneity. To such a writer, it will seem very important that his novel should be conspicuously of its time and in the mode. The trouble is that his idea of 'the time' and 'the mode' may be partly derived from some recent novel or novels that have caught the public fancy. His efforts to be contemporary will then lead him into a more or less uninspired copying of these.

But he'll miss the boat. The writing and publishing of books is, in general, a slow business. It takes as long to produce a book as it does to produce a baby : a finished manuscript that's handed in to a publisher today won't be in the bookshops for the best part of a year.

Let us suppose that some brilliant novelist, being closely and instinctively in touch with the mental currents of his time, hits upon the idea for some new and sharply topical kind of novel. He then has to write it, and it then has to be published; and these processes will take, say, eighteen months. During the three further months that follow its publication, this novel will become immensely popular by virtue of its topicality, its of-the-moment quality. Thereupon, a great many people will decide to climb on to the bandwagon; and about a year later, the publisher's reader will be inundated with imitations—good imitations, in many cases—of that original trend-setting novel. Some of these will, after a further nine or twelve months, be published. But if you add up these various periods of time, you will perceive that these imitations will have come on to the market not much less than three years after the first man hit upon an idea, an approach that was then a topical novelty. During that period, the pot will probably have gone off the boil. Some of those derived or para-sitical novels will sell sufficiently; but at the best, they will be followers rather than pioneers, and instead of the sharp con-temporaneity that their authors pursued so keenly, they will have an air of being dated.

Beware, therefore, of the following fallacy: "Everybody seems to be writing novels of type XYZ, and they're very trendy and very popular and very profitable. Why shouldn't I write one too?" To think on these lines is to invite the failure of staleness.

The point can be illustrated by reference to the early novels of Kingsley Amis. In their day, these were highly original; and they were not written in obedience to current fashion or in response to any theory about what the public wanted. On the contrary, they arose out of something like a private joke, cherished secretly between Mr Amis and his friends, not considered likely to have any wider appeal. But they did have a wider appeal, and soon *That Uncertain Feeling* and *Lucky Jim* had become trend-setters. This did not prevent them from being excellent books; but it inflicted a heavy and (for the most part) an unprofitable burden upon publishers' readers. For some years afterwards, every post would bring in another sham-Amis novel, written by somebody who was excitedly eager to climb on to the bandwagon but lacked the master's talent. It is not over yet: even now, one's heart can sink as one opens a typescript and finds, within the first few pages, the too-familiar properties of the *genre*. We meet some young lout, living in the drab provinces, grammar-school-educated, chip on shoulder, at odds with his proletarian father, working in most cases for the local paper or (occasionally) teaching: he will grin and grimace over beer, he will pick his nose and fart, he will make ludicrous seduction-attempts, he will carry on about Jazz and 'The Establishment', he will go in for obsessive buffoonery and disastrous japes, and nothing in his whole story will fail to be entirely familiar and predictable.

It would be too much to say flatly that you must not, on any account, write this story again. But if you do, it had better be good.

There are a number of other novels about which the same can be said. They are perfectly sound in themselves, but they have been written—and in some cases published—rather too often. It's a shade rash to write them again, unless you can do it very well.

Here are some further examples, some novels or novel-elements that have become clichés:

(i) The imaginative reconstruction of a remote past, prehistoric or mythological, as understood in the light of archaeology, anthropology, and comparative religion. This is a highbrow *genre*, calling for a certain amount of background study. At its best it makes magnificent reading, and notably in the hands of its high priestess, Mary Renault; but she and others have set an alarmingly high standard. The great mistake is to regard it as a soft option. When this kind of novel fails to be outstanding, it tends to be rubbish: the colourful background and properties draw attention to any central imaginative weakness, rather than making up for it.

(ii) A more lowbrow version of the same thing. A grand rowdy mix-up of sex, violence, and religion in some ancient world, real or imagined: gladiators, bosoms, toppling disasters, temples and sinister priesthoods with their rituals and their schemings: slave-girls being whipped to death. Much is commonly made of the fact that in a society conceived on these lines, people can be plausibly represented as not wearing many clothes, and also as carrying swords and spears all the time, with little public restraint upon the use thereof.

Sometimes we are taken right back to cave-man days, with uncouth characters called Ug and Pong spearing one another and having babies in ditches and stumbling about in swamps and forests. It can be good fun if you're in the mood.

(iii) The novel that is too simply and thinly derived from the fact that its author read English Literature at his university. Often he was a poet or novelist by vocation, but then had to go into some dismal job because he had a family to feed and couldn't get much money by writing. Typically, he became a copy-writer in an advertising agency: the point and tension of this story—which is plainly an autobiographical complaint—arises from the fact that while this job was, in a way, related to the author's education and ambitions, it also involved some loss to his integrity, his bright vision.

In another version that's commonly American, this becomes the campus-novel : the faculty-members who occupy the foreground invariably have Literature for their field, never Biochemistry or Economics.

Literary studies at university level tend to generate a particular kind of stress or disappointment in later years. The same may be true of other fields of study; but where Literature is concerned at least, this is over-familiar territory to the publisher's reader.

(iv) The politico-military thriller of tough action, *unless* it takes the following principles into account : (a) If there ever were any 'atom secrets', we don't believe in them now : we find it hard to believe in military secrets of any sort. (b) Nobody believes in a dualistic world any more, with Good Us in total and righteous opposition to Bad Them. (c) We shall take it for granted that the Organisation—the one that employs your conscience-harrowed agent—is blind and absurd. If your story is to depend upon his gradual and upsetting discovery of this, you have to account for his stupidity in not seeing it from the start. (d) You won't be able to curdle our blood with any newly-invented bomb, gun, ray, germ, or whatever. We're too hardened.

(v) The painfully Irish novel. Glory and heartbreak of wild uproarious youth in Dublin, with students and poets and poverty and fine whirling talk, and Guinness and the Gardai, and people being sick at parties, and mad-eyed mistresses and dotty peers, and great crumbling Georgian mansions where pigs loiter in the drawing-rooms, and everybody hallooing off into the night in some overloaded rackety old car, while the inescapable Church hovers over all.

(vi) The painfully American novel, in which everybody makes a full-time job of acting out—in roaring titanic fashion—some rôle selected from a Jung-styled repertoire of ancient myths and symbols. This is sometimes a poetical and prophetical lament for the world's despair and for the hellishness (erroneously seen as total) of modern American life; sometimes it's a great raw bleeding slice of history, full of violence and filth. Sometimes it's both.

Two things tend to be wrong with Americans, affecting their novels disadvantageously. One is that they worry too much about being American: the other is that they take book-psychology much too seriously.

(vii) The holiday novel. How I—a nice English schoolmarm —was quite bowled over by the hot Mediterranean sun and the garlic and the bottom-pinching Italians.

(viii) The satirical *danse macabre*: a derisive rattling of dry puppets, a jubilantly sick capering through vistas of dimness, inspired by a vision of 'modern society' as corrupt (obviously), and also as phoney and daft in the highest degree, and indeed as actually dead, though unaware of the fact. There is usually some suggestion of nostalgia for grand colourful old *reality*, which is there all the time, if only people had the energy to reach out for it.

Smugness is the fault of this novel: its writer tends to be young and censorious.

(ix) The solemn and weighty D.Porn. thesis, in which the service of Venus is endlessly described in detail, and is made to seem like a necessary but very unpleasant kind of medical treatment.

(x) The young girl's novel about how I got seduced.

(xi) The young girl's novel about how I didn't get seduced.

(xii) The agonised Catholic novel about birth control. This is always written by a lady.

(xiii) The agonised Catholic novel about clerical celibacy. This is never written by a priest.

(xiv) The female novel which is too simply a complaint about how beastly men are to girls. You're right, dear; but it isn't a new discovery.

(xv) The novel that is based too simply upon this further fact: that *each* sex can, with some plausibility, accuse the other of being essentially predatory in amorous relationships.

(xvi) The novel that is based too simply upon the end of adolescent self-centredness and the learning of compassion.

Usually it involves the late and upsetting discovery that this girl isn't just a luscious sex-machine but an actual human being as well, despite appearances.

(xvii) The novel that brings a group of strangers together in some confined and stressful environment for a prolonged ordeal, so that their shams and acts collapse and it becomes apparent what they *really* are.

(xviii) The army novel: though the English version of this has become rarer since conscription ended. It depends upon the conflict or tension between a young recruit who's cultured and sensitive and a bull-necked sergeant who isn't. Its weakness is that it tends to labour the obvious. War is a barbaric and irrational business, and if there are to be armies at all, they plainly can't be run on civilised and reasonable lines. Your discovery that the army is not so run is very far from being a new one: don't proclaim it too excitedly.

(xix) The psycho-clinical case-history. The writer of this novel supposes himself to have achieved the whole of a novelist's task if he has successfully conveyed to us the nature and flavour of (say) schizophrenic experience. It tends to be fascinating, in an awful way, since we're all amateur psychologists; but it seldom works as a novel.

(xx) The vast family chronicle, with a family tree that unfolds at the back and tends to get torn. It begins with old Josiah Heckthornthwaite, who indomitably founded the Mill in 1762, and who now glares down in disapproval, from his dark portrait on the boardroom wall, upon the disintegration of the modern world and the scruffy antics of the young.

(xxi) The novel that devotes all its energies to playing elaborate games with the novel-convention. As a novelist, you are fully entitled to be clever in any way that takes your fancy and lies within your powers; but don't *overact* the part of the man who, writing a clever novel, builds it around the character of a clever novelist, in whose work he himself features, and writes a novel that is in fact *this* one, the one that you're now reading, so that the narrator becomes a character within a novel written by a 'himself' who is (in a sense) a quasi-fictitious character in a novel not written by anybody, except that . . . After a certain amount of this, we all run lunatic and drop the book.

Each of these games has been played very often indeed, and possibly by yourself. If the novel that you wrote last year falls into one of the categories just listed, don't take it too personally: you aren't the only one.

You may be tempted to despair: at times, it does seem that every possible novel has been written too often already. Seldom indeed does the publisher's reader find a typescript that cannot be described in terms of earlier novels.

You probably cannot hope to avoid clichés altogether. But bear in mind that they are clichés: that response of "oh, not *again*!" will only be elicited if you present them raw, as though they had just been thought of for the first time and needed to be proclaimed. Do something with them: put them across in terms of an experience or vision that's very much your own. "The great artists," says Maupassant, "are those who impose their particular illusions upon humanity." Develop this experience, this vision, maybe this illusion: look intense upon life and people, and with your own eyes, until you become very much aware of what a character in *Point Counter Point* calls "the astonishingness of the most obvious things." G. K. Chesterton was an expert on this astonishingness: his usefulness to the writer is underrated at this time, chiefly because of his stylistic perversity. He is worth studying.

On originality, Maupassant may be allowed to have the last word. "Everything contains some element of the unexplored because we are accustomed to use our eyes only with the memory of what other people before us have thought about the object we are looking at . . . In order to describe a fire burning or a tree in a field, let us stand in front of that fire or that tree until they no longer look to us like any other fire or any other tree. That is how one becomes original."

Stare at that fire and that tree, and don't read too much. General bookishness can be a definite handicap to the novelist, and so can our civilisation's preference for secondhand or derived experience of every kind. A novelist writes, as a painter paints, with eyes rather than with hands; and eyes were never meant for looking at print, as any oculist will tell you.

CHAPTER SIX

TO CARE AND NOT TO CARE

THE ASPIRING WRITER, perplexed by failure, often casts about for some kind of formula that will define the requirements of the market. His own novel has been rejected : in a brief kindly letter, the publishers explained that it was not quite what they wanted. Well, what *did* they want? What *were* they looking for?

So far as the various kinds and classifications of novel are concerned, one can work out limited answers to such questions. Study lists and announcements, and it will soon become clear that Messrs X are looking for pornographic thrillers and Messrs Y for rarefied highbrow brain-teasers. But this does not take us very far. Most good publishers are broadminded about *genre* but fastidious about quality : to the question "What are you looking for?" they could only reply "*Good* novels." And there isn't any overall formula by which this merit that they're seeking might be defined.

You must not, therefore, expect the publisher's reader to be able to tell you what he's looking for when he first opens your typescript at its first page. The fact is that he isn't looking for anything at all : he is submitting himself to a process, an experience, a treatment, with a view to its subsequent explanation and evaluation. At this first moment, his mind is a complete blank, and it's up to you to work upon it.

Disappointingly to some people, this means that there's no point in approaching him for a hot tip about specific requirements. In a sense, he is comparable to a theatrical talent-scout, but he hasn't been briefed in advance and told what to find. He very seldom goes out to find anything. The fictional part of a

97

publisher's list is not designed in advance, on some basis of pre-conceived themes and treatments: it is assembled from the best of what actually turns up. So don't come up to me at a party with a question of this kind: "Treacle-wells have been in the news just lately, and I've half-written a novel that's entirely set in a treacle-well. Do you think that Messrs XYZ would want it? Are they *looking* for treacle-well novels?"

Stick to your task: finish the novel, and make it a good one. Don't hunt for specific requirements, apart from that one question of quality. The publisher's reader has no preconceptions at all. Work upon him.

You will need to make some kind of a positive impression at a fairly early stage. In literary experience as well as in personal relationships, first impressions are very often decisive, and there's a bad outlook for the novel that only reveals its charms at a late stage or after several readings. An early and definite *bite* is neces-sary—not only because its absence will generate an initial and possibly decisive boredom in the publisher's reader, but also because novels tend (within limits) to sell on their opening pages. If you doubt this, make a brief point-of-sale study of the actual market. Go to some bookshop or library, and watch people browsing and choosing. Their eye will terd to get caught by a jacket, a title, an author's name; and there'll often be a cursory glance at the blurb, a vague thumbing through. But in a great many cases, the moment of decision will be reached by way of an experimental reading of the first sequence, the first few pages. If the potential customer then feels himself to be hooked and drawn in, he will buy or borrow, as the case may be; if not, he will lose interest and put the book back on the shelves.

The point is an obvious one. People aren't obliged to read your novel, and they won't bother unless they find the exercise a rewarding one. At *every* stage, therefore, you must provide them with an incentive: their attention and interest must be caught decisively at the beginning, sustained and developed throughout, and (at the end) resolved and released in some way that will give an agreeable sense of finality. The rewards offered at these various stages may well be very different : your book may start as light social comedy and then deepen progressively into metaphysical tragedy. But *some* kind of reward must always be on offer, and especially in these decisive first pages.

You start off with the odds in your favour. People open novels, as they attend parties, with a general expectation and intention of being pleased : given half a chance, your readers are very willing to enjoy and appreciate everything that you provide. But this initial goodwill justifies no kind of complacency on your part : you have to work upon it, you have to exploit it and develop it. Do this successfully in your opening pages, and the author-reader relationship will get off to a very good start : a kind of momentum will be established, and if necessary, this will carry the relationship on, through some relatively dull territory that comes later. But if the dullness comes first, it will dissipate that vague initial goodwill, provoking a hostile response that may be disastrous.

In polishing and perfecting your novel for publication, you must therefore pay special attention to the beginning. Here, in any case, you will come up against some of your thorniest difficulties. In these first pages, the requirements of movement and action will clash with the requirements of clarity and comprehension, and you'll want to have it both ways. You'll hardly want to bore your readers with a slow beginning in the nineteenth-century style, a leisurely spacious introduction to your various characters and their backgrounds; on the other hand, if you plunge into action at once, you're very likely to arouse bewilderment, and you may have to slow down awkwardly and explain yourself sheepishly at a somewhat later stage. This often happens in ill-made novels : a good beginning, with plenty of life and attack, is followed by a sharp anti-climax, a patch of grievously slack water. The readers have to stand by while the novelist extricates himself from the confusion generated by an opening sequence that was otherwise excellent.

"The disadvantage of the dramatic opening," said Ford

Madox Ford, "is that after the dramatic passage is done you have to go back to getting your characters in, a proceeding that the reader is apt to dislike. The danger with the reflective opening is that the reader is apt to miss being gripped at once by the story. Openings are therefore of necessity affairs of compromise."

This compromise may be an easier matter than it was, since the modern reader is accustomed to a method more poetical and suggestive than was usual in the nineteenth-century novel: he isn't so heavily dependent upon having everything squarely set forth and fully explained. He can take a hint. In our time, the novelist has taken over a good deal of the territory that used to belong to the poet, and he can very often proceed in something like a poet's manner: where beginnings are concerned, this means that he can usually resolve that compromise, without danger, in the dramatic rather than the reflective way. Two thousand years ago, Horace recommended the poet to plunge straight in; more recently, the same principle was at once stated and enacted by Sir John Henry Moore:

"I hate a prologue to a story
  Worse than the tuning of a fiddle,
    Squeaking and dinning;
  Hang order and connection,
  I love to dash into the middle;
    Exclusive of the fame and glory,
  There is a comfort on reflection
    To think you've done with the beginning.

"And so at supper one fine night,
    Hearing a cry of Alla, Alla,
  The Prince was damnably confounded,
    And in a fright,
  But more so when he saw himself surrounded
  By fifty Turks; and at their head the fierce Abdalla."

You can usually start a present-day novel with this kind of briskness: only exceptionally will it be necessary for you to explain to us, first of all, who the Prince was, and where the fifty Turks had come from, and what historical grievances made Abdalla so fierce. But in so far as they need to be known at all, these things should become apparent fairly soon : you can very usefully tease our curiosity for a time, but you must not frustrate it.

The main thing, at this early stage, is that you should show a certain consideration for the reader. You know about this novel that's now beginning : he doesn't. Don't let him flounder about in perplexity; give him a chance to see what kind of commodity is on offer and what kind of response is intended. Various hares will be started in these first pages : discreetly, let him know which are the ones that need to be followed. Try to anticipate, and to prevent, misapprehensions and false starts : guide us with a little extra care until we've found our way and can look after ourselves. Often, after a very attentive reading of the first fifty pages of a novel, the publisher's reader suddenly realises in astonishment that the thing is meant to be *funny*; or conversely, that it *isn't* meant to be funny.

There are a number of particular mistakes that need to be avoided here : more precisely, there are a number of techniques —ways of beginning a novel—that show a marked tendency to prove unsuccessful.

Chief among these is the boding and mystificatory opening, full of dark ominous allusions to matters so far unexplained and unknown. Properly handled, this can work splendidly : it can act as a kind of overture, establishing an emotional key that will be taken up again at a much later stage, after intervening passages in very different keys. It can also plant crucial facts in the reader's mind, where they will lie forgotten until they're summoned up to take their place in the final pattern. The slow deep sad Prologue to *Romeo and Juliet,* followed at once by a quick sparrow-twitter and dog-scuffle in the streets, is an example of how well this kind of beginning can function on the stage.

But it needs careful handling. Mere mood-music, aiming only at the generation of a specific emotional atmosphere, is a difficult thing to write; and curiosity, like hunger, is only an agreeable sensation when there's at least a prospect that it will be satisfied reasonably soon. In less-than-expert hands, a novel that begins in this fashion will very often irritate the reader instead of intriguing him. Don't let him feel that he's being gratuitously mystified. Your purpose must be concealed. At least one-half of the novelist's task lies in the arbitrary working-up of interest and curiosity, but this fact needs to be camouflaged: deceptively, the novelist must always *seem* anxious to tell, to inform, to enlighten. The convention has to be maintained. He is guiding his readers through a dark forest, and they must suppose it to be real: he mustn't be seen erecting it by stage-carpentry in order to fool them. He must not appear to mystify.

It is another dangerous tactic to start off with a deceptively trite or simple picture, which you then intend to develop progressively in various directions. This often happens with the novel that has been constructed on lines too theoretical, insufficiently organic; and the final effect is very often excellent. But this final effect will only be seen by a reader who presses on to the end. The publisher's reader will do this, since he's paid to: the ordinary reader will be alienated by the thin emptiness of the beginning and he will lay the book aside, never suspecting what delayed-action riches he has missed.

The reader must always be provided with some kind of an incentive. Your novel's most serious point and effect may very well depend upon something that will only become apparent at the very end, or even after a number of readings; but unless you already have a great reputation, you cannot expect your readers to take this on faith, plodding on wearily in the sure and certain hope that it's all going to be worth it in the end. Secondary attractions must be provided in such cases, tasty meats to nourish us on our pilgrimage.

When they're speaking privately and off the record, a surprising number of writers are prepared to say boldly—and even defiantly—that nobody can hope to understand or enjoy their novels at all except on the basis of a deep familiarity that can only be gained from several readings. But if it's really like this, the publisher will seldom want to bet on many people volunteering for so lengthy a discipline, unless the author's reputation guarantees their ultimate reward.

It is also rash to begin a novel with a series of wholly disconnected episodes, each one introducing a separate character in his own environment, or maybe a group of characters : the whole series being combined later on into some joint action or development. The danger here is of scrappiness, of attention dispersed where it could more fruitfully be concentrated, of a slow start to the actual novel. Such a method can succeed : much more usually, it fails. You are always on thin ice, in fact, whenever there's a total break in your novel's continuity, with completely new characters introduced in an unfamiliar setting. At such a moment, the reader will be bothered by the relationship between this new material and what's gone before. This bother and tension in his mind can be fruitful; but unless it's relieved fairly quickly, it can harden into irritation. A large number of such breaks or discontinuities, at the very beginning of your novel, are a luxury that you are unlikely to afford.

The audience have come to watch you perform (say) a scientific experiment; and they'll get bored and fidgety if, after they've come into the hall, you keep them waiting while you set up the apparatus, muttering lame explanations as you do so. They want some action. Have everything set up before you invite them in.

When they do come into the hall, take care not to begin by confusing them. Don't let your first few pages contain too many characters, insufficiently differentiated. If at some crowded party you are introduced very rapidly to a great many strangers, their various names and their grinning faces will start to slip and coalesce in your mind : you won't have met any of them effectively. Don't let this happen to the reader of your novel : don't let him flounder in perplexity through these first sequences, furrowing his brow, turning back all the time to find out once again whether 'Tom' was the rich uncle or the trouble-making son or the pussy-cat. Until we've found our feet and got moving, let there be a certain simplicity, a clarity of labelling: help us along with kindly hints. We're strangers here.

Even so, you must get things moving. Of all the unkind remarks that tend to recur in readers' reports, one of the commonest is to the effect that the novel in question gets off to a slow start. In the course of revision, put your novel into the dock and see how plausibly it can be defended from an accusation of this kind. Does it get moving in the first few pages? Is there a general feeling, from the start, of something considerable that's now beginning? A sense of opening out, of broadening, of possibilities? Is the reader made to feel that he has actually embarked upon a voyage of exploration and discovery?

Don't let him hang around for too long at the point of departure, while you fiddle with the baggage and the maps and the arrangements. Get the show on the road.

Your problem, at this stage, is the problem of getting us interested, so that we shall *want* to come along with you. It might seem desirable, then, to pay some attention to the social and psychological phenomenon of novel-reading. What kind of pleasure and profit are you trying to give, what need is it that you are attempting to meet? Why do people read novels at all? When you come to think of it, there's no obvious reason why they should: a man from Mars, resembling us but lacking a human psychology, might think it very odd and surprising that a rational creature should choose to dissipate part of his short precious life in reading a series of untrue statements about non-existent people.

With this fascinating enigma, the novelist need not be concerned: he can rest quite comfortably and securely upon the fact that people *do* like reading stories, if only because of their insatiable curiosity about other people. You get them interested by arousing this curiosity, with some promise that it will then be satisfied. This is the rock-bottom art of fiction: the novel can do infinitely more than this, but it won't succeed at all if it does less. "Curiosity becomes the more eager from the incompleteness

of the first information," says George Eliot, in words that constitute your first commandment; and Forster tells us that the novel,
considered as a story, can only have one merit—"that of making
the audience want to know what happens next."

But it is not merely a question of knowing, of factual curiosity
about the course of events: if it were, we could hardly read the
same novel a second time, or not until we had forgotten our first
reading. In practice, it doesn't work out like that. If a novel has
any quality at all, we are tempted to turn back from the last
page and begin all over again, at once or after a very short
interval; and this second reading will commonly be more rewarding than the first, even though the element of mere curiosity and
surprise is—to say the least—a great deal weaker. We know
what's coming, this time, as the astonishing *dénouement* draws
nearer; and for this reason, we are all the better able to appreciate and enjoy its quality of surprisingness, even though it is no
longer (in any literal sense) an actual surprise. We relish the
journey, not merely the arrival.

And so, while in a rock-bottom sense the story-teller is concerned to arouse our curiosity, he is in a more crucial sense
concerned to arouse our interest. We need, basically, to wonder
what's going to happen next: more seriously, we need to *care*
about what's going to happen next—even if, by reason of an
earlier reading, we already know what it's going to be. Involvement is the thing.

When we read the newspapers, our mood for the most part
is one of mild curiosity: we're willing enough to know what's
going on, and we're stimulated mildly by the jumble of doubtful
and unrelated happenings, but it all seems a little remote. But
then we come across some item, some news story, that directly
concerns ourselves or our interests, and at once our attention is
heightened: our factual curiosity continues, but now we have
started to care.

From the start, the novelist has to arouse that kind of attention: his reader has to care. It is well known that his caring will
often be fostered if he is allowed to identify with some principal

character, and if he thus becomes comparable to the newspaper-reader who has discovered a paragraph about himself.

But a wider principle is involved, and very crucially. Boredom is always highly infectious; and frequently though not always, the same goes for interest. The teacher who's bored with his subject will infallibly set the class yawning: the teacher who's in love with his subject will very often communicate that passion, or some part of it, to the least responsive of his pupils. From our own schooldays, we can all remember the profit and the loss that we derived from both aspects of this phenomenon.

If you want people to be interested and involved in your novel, the overwhelmingly important thing is that you yourself should be interested and involved in it, and in all the various characters and happenings and visions and emotions contained within it. This will not guarantee success, but a lack of interest will certainly guarantee failure. C. S. Lewis made the point well: "Write about what really interests you, whether it is real things or imaginary things, and nothing else. (Notice this means that if you are interested *only* in writing you will never be a writer, because you will have nothing to write about.)"

This may seem a point too obvious to need emphasis: who on earth is going to submit to the endless drudgery of writing a novel, if he isn't really in love with the project and with everything in it? But unfortunately, many people seem to do exactly that: they write novels under motivations that are only tenuously related to any real personal caring.

This is one of the facts that bring tedium into the life of a publisher's reader. Again and again, he comes across the novel that wasn't loved by its mother, and is a feeble puny thing in consequence. In such a case, every page will have the weary plausibility of disliked memory; the story will be told with grim fidelity, as though in reluctant but honourable fulfilment of a rashly-given promise. Such an author seems bored with his subject-matter: so far from wishing to engage closely with it, he seems anxious to keep it at arm's length and then drop it as soon as possible.

Such negative attitudes are indeed infectious. The reader comes to agree with the author, and wants to drop the subject and the book.

This is quite a common phenomenon, and one can only guess at what lies behind it. Perhaps the author had some kind of pre-conception about what kind of book he ought to write, some theory about what the public wanted. Such ideas are dangerous: the wisest thing is to follow your own vocation and write the novel that you most authentically *want* to write, the one that interests *you* most deeply, ignoring all preconceptions and theories. The infection will spread: you will then arouse other people's interest, unless other factors keep it asleep or frighten it away.

In this respect, your own reading-habits will provide a useful pointer, if honestly assessed. Consider the kind of novel that you read most eagerly for its own sake, in your unbuttoned moments, when nobody's looking: it will not necessarily be the same as the novel that you praise in sophisticated company, or read in solemn purposeful fashion for self-improvement. These more inward and genuine tastes will provide at least a rough suggestion of the kind of novel that you can most realistically propose to write, the lines along which—being interested yourself—you are most likely to interest other people.

In the sad pathology of the novel, these cases recur: the books that were not loved by their mothers, and therefore grew up unlovable. One can sometimes diagnose an effort at psycho-therapy, a reluctant attention to something nasty in the mind; one can often diagnose a bad choice of *genre*, an imprecise fol-lowing of vocation. But sometimes the trouble appears to be more serious. What if you cast about to discover the things that interest you most deeply, and discover that you aren't really very much interested in anything? It does happen: boredom, *ennui*, apathy, *accidia* are alternative names for a disease very wide-spread in the twentieth century, "fear in a handful of dust", a principal theme in *The Waste Land*. If this is your trouble, you will probably be unwise to take up novel-writing, or any other occupation that involves an endless picking at the dried-up brain. Evelyn Waugh bears witness to the fact that you might succeed, but also to the fact that you'll be venturing into dangerous and unhappy territory. Bouts of periodical apathy or depression affect us all, and for the most part they soon pass. But one frequently encounters a novel that suggests a total apathy towards everything on the author's part, not merely an apathy towards his present task and subject-matter. Such a novel has to be put out of its misery as soon as possible.

The trouble is that bored and lonely people often feel a strong compulsion to write. As subject-matter, apathy can be useful and (in its way) fascinating : as a state of mind in the novelist, it is disastrous.

If you are to arouse and retain the interest of the publisher's reader, and subsequently of the larger public, you need therefore to be engaged or involved with your characters and their story.

This engagement, this involvement will commonly need to have what can only be called a moral element. This does not mean that your novel needs to preach a sermon, or to be written in a spirit of censoriousness. But if you are to be interesting about what people do and what happens to them, you must possess and convey some kind of feeling that these things *matter* : you must have what Joyce Cary called "an ordered attitude" towards the great emotional drives like ambition and love, and towards the various ways in which they can work out in practice.

Sexual behaviour offers the most obvious example of this. In so far as society moves towards total permissiveness, and towards a total acceptance of this in people's minds, it simply ceases to be interesting whether A goes to bed with B or not. Who cares? Copulation is widely believed to be enjoyable; it is interesting to the pathological *voyeur*, and also (in a different way) to the doctor and the professional sexologist. But to the novelist in his professional capacity, it is not interesting or useful at all unless it involves relationships and possibilities that matter, working out in ways that are happy or disastrous, desirable or hateful. In sexual and in other matters, a society wholly governed by permissive indifference (if such a society can be imagined) would give him nothing to get his teeth into : conversely, he has always been richly nourished by any society that's full of complex taboos and prohibitions.

It's just as well for the novelist that our own society has not travelled as far as many people suppose in the direction of total permissiveness, total indifference, total absence of moral structure. It probably can't go very far in that direction without losing its motivations and therefore dying altogether. But it certainly offers less useful material to the story-teller than did the more highly structured (if technologically simpler) societies of two or three generations ago.

The novelist needs his ordered attitudes, his sense of what matters in human life. Many people feel, however, that all such ordered and morally structured attitudes are, in this age, out of the question : they have become intellectually untenable, or at least they are grossly out of fashion. Hence, there arises a strong tendency for novelists to write from a standpoint of satirical anarchy, hurling derision in all directions at once, joyously or furiously undermining every possible kind of ordered attitude, asserting chaos. The result can work, and very soundly, as headlong farce or as harrowing nightmare.

But in less-than-brilliant hands, it can also be an enormous bore, and it very frequently is. The point that needs to be remembered is that anything in the nature of satire depends for its functioning upon the writer having some implied platform or position of his own. The strict and confident moralist can laugh or weep at human foolishness, his own included; but neither the laughter nor the tears are possible unless the foolishness can be recognised and defined by contrast with some kind of possible wisdom. Unless you have an idea of goodness, you cannot say that any man or any happening is bad, and you cannot therefore tell a story that will seem to matter. Moral anarchy and nihilism may or may not be imposed upon us by the ruthless logic of experience; but without any doubt at all, such outlooks are imaginatively sterile. The conclusion that they point to is not that you should write an anarchic or nihilistic kind of novel, but rather that you shouldn't write a novel at all, or anything else. You should cut your throat, or just lie on the carpet and bellow.

General protests and denunciations, hurled indiscriminately in all directions and from no particular standpoint, end up by saying nothing at all. Blasphemy is not possible in a totally and authentically atheistic society : you can't be off-beat unless there's a beat for you to be off. These things function by contrast.

Mauriac once asserted that the modern novel is in a bad way, and that the trouble arises "from the conception of man held by the present generation : a conception that is totally negative". "The collapse of the novel," he said on the same occasion, "is due to the destruction of this fundamental concept : the awareness of good and evil." It certainly seems that the Catholic novelist, or any other who writes from within a highly-structured system of values and morality, has an unfair advantage over the rest : though he may not use this advantage wisely or at all.

The aspiring novelist will hardly go running off to seek instruction from Father O'Blimp for the sake of acquiring a professional qualification. But he will do well to sort out his own attitudes, his own various ideas of the desirable—as distinct from the probable—in human life. He will then be more able to avoid the dullness of the writer who just says "Hell is murky"— whether gleefully or miserably—and then underlines that boring fact again and again, devoting all his attention to twists and curlicues and tortuous variations in the underlining.

Emotionally and morally, the novelist therefore needs to be involved in the story that he's telling : apathy and nihilism will kill it stone-dead, and the publisher's reader will yawn over its flat pages.

It is a shade less obvious, perhaps, that a novel can also be ruined by too deep and passionate an involvement on the author's part. If your feelings about your subject-matter are frantic and agonised, you may find it very hard to concentrate with sufficient detachment upon the task of writing; and your book may end up as a wild outpouring, deserving a kind of human respect, but quite unpublishable.

To many people, this comes as a hard and unacceptable lesson. If you are in some kind of tense anguish—about the world's condition, maybe, or about your own—you may find it hard to think about anything else : you may even feel that it would be an ignoble thing, an act of evasion or escapism, if you *did* think about anything else. So situated, you may well deserve sympathy or praise or both : it doesn't at all follow that you will be well placed for writing a novel. Authenticity in your own experience, and in your own response to it, is not enough : the craftsman's task still remains, and this will usually call for a certain detachment, a certain distance.

Repeatedly, the publisher's reader encounters the novel that amounts to a huge and valid chunk of emotion, a great raw jagged red-hot bleeding lump of experience, which cannot conceivably be published : the author has not even begun to consider seriously, and much less to attempt, the particular kind of work that's involved when you convert raw material into a marketable literary artefact. This is a common kind of failure, arising perhaps from a romantic illusion about what writing is : an excessive emphasis upon writing as therapy and self-expression, an inadequate emphasis upon writing as craftsmanship. The author's tumultuous self is put across all right, with all its troubles; but it comes across so tumultuously that the poor novel gets crushed.

The fact is that it is usually necessary to get your subject-matter more or less under emotional control before you can do anything useful with it : though a very powerful talent may make this unnecessary. Poetry, according to Wordsworth, is "emotion recollected in tranquillity"; and until you achieve at least the beginnings of that tranquillity, you will hardly find it possible to manage the emotion. A poem like *In Memoriam* can immortalise grief, remaining palpably authentic and very moving for ever; but it will seldom be written under the first paralysing bang of bereavement.

"The greatest intensity in art in all its shapes," says Truman Capote, "is achieved with a deliberate, hard, and cool head."

A great many novels fail for this reason. To their authors, this advice can be given : write about something in which your feelings are less uncontrollably involved. "Teach us to care and not to care," said Eliot, addressing God : in your novel, let there be engagement and also detachment.

Remember that you're trying to please the publisher's reader with your literary presence; and remember that the roaring, obsessed, self-pitying, revelatory bore is quite impossible company.

CHAPTER SEVEN

PARTY MANNERS

MILE AFTER MILE through desert and jungle, the publisher's reader presses on, deep into the heart of your novel. He's paid—though not lavishly—to do it, and he's a man of immense honour and integrity: he isn't going to skip.

You want him to be happy; you want him to finish this novel with a certain regret that it's over, and to mention the fact in his report, so that as well as having this book accepted, you are implored to write another. Already (let us hope) you have secured his initial attention, his initial goodwill, by the aptness and bite of your opening pages: this favourable situation must now be sustained and developed over a long period. He has to find you tolerable company, to say the least of it, and not merely for those first few moments.

Not all of us find it easy to be tolerable company, in the flesh or on paper; and if we find it difficult, theoretical study won't always mend matters. The art of pleasing is a concrete and empirical affair; literary acceptability, like social acceptability, is chiefly a matter of tact and personality and convention, of sound instinct and good training and bitter experience. The problem of pleasing the readers of your novel has a lot in common with the problem of pleasing the people you meet socially.

The parallel is a good one: of the advice that needs to be given to the aspiring novelist, a substantial proportion is very like the advice given in books about etiquette and social behaviour. But there is one great difference. Since childhood, we have all been accustomed to the problems of personal and social relationship, and we can handle them with some degree of assurance: except in extreme cases, most of us know fairly well how to behave at a party, if we hope to be invited a second time. It becomes a matter of instinct, and we adjust easily to the very different requirements of different occasions. But when we first approach the writing of a novel, we're in an unfamiliar *milieu* and we're attempting an unfamiliar kind of relationship : we tend to blunder about and make fools of ourselves.

The aspiring novelist is comparable, therefore, not to party-guests in general but rather to some shy and gauche young man from the outback, who is just entering upon society for the first time and doesn't quite know how to comport himself. If such a young man gives offence and is not invited again, the reasons for this will often be closely analogous to a publisher's reasons for rejecting a novel. If you want to be acceptable, you must learn to please other people, or at least to avoid the danger of offending them too grossly; and 'other people', as we all know, are an awkward and irrational crowd, needing to be handled carefully on lines that don't always make theoretical sense.

Books on etiquette and behaviour are, unfortunately, of limited value : popularity and social success will only exceptionally be the direct consequence of studious attention to their pages. Instinct, background, and experience are usually the decisive factors. Nevertheless, there are a number of golden rules that can usefully be borne in mind, by the uncertain party-guest and by the aspiring novelist as well. Here are some of them.

(i) *"Don't lecture people."* On any social occasion, it is heartbreaking indeed to see the innocent youth who holds forth, informs, explains, asserts, and in general lectures anybody who will submit to the treatment. Most people drift away from him, but there will usually be one rabbit-eyed girl who cannot escape. Mesmerised, she stands there, while the torrent flows. That young man won't be asked again; or at least, not until he has learnt that there's a time and a place for everything.

If he's very young, he may be bewildered by the company's response to his behaviour : he may point out, indignantly, that his lecture was a very true and important and topical one. People *should* have been prepared to listen to it. In this claim, he may conceivably be justified; but this won't alter the social facts of the matter.

A great many novels fail because they contain a didactic or informative element that's far too strong, and has not been duly subordinated to the novelist's prime task of pleasing by narrative. In extreme cases, one often suspects that the author didn't really want to write a novel at all: his genuine desire was to write something like an argumentative book or article or essay. If he had a desire of that kind, he was in a difficulty with which we can have all sympathy: there isn't the market that there was a generation or two ago for amateur philosophisings, for generally didactic or argumentative writing by non-specialists. You may have some very excellent arguments and opinions and theories: you may believe that the world needs to hear them, and in this you may quite possibly be right. If you are a qualified and recognised expert on the subject in question, you should find it possible to get into print, and to deliver your lecture in the right place—that is to say, in the lecture-hall. And if you are merely a celebrity, a big name in some different field, you may have the same good fortune, while deserving it less. But otherwise you will probably find it difficult to secure a workable pulpit or platform for your lecturings. This is a pity: we're all too much at the mercy of experts and specialists nowadays, and we could do with that amateur lecture of yours. But the facts of the market-place have to be faced.

The danger arises if you coerce into the novel-form materials and ideas and preoccupations that didn't want to take that form at all and weren't at ease with it. This happens constantly: it is a prime cause of novels being rejected.

The narrative instinct and the didactic or informative instinct are very different things and are not easily compatible: there's only a slender market nowadays for the novel that stages a philosophical house-party, after the style of Huxley or Mallock, with endless deep discussions over the wine. "I don't care for philosophers in books," says Joyce Cary. "They are always bores. A novel should be an experience and convey an emotional truth rather than an argument." "I do not even think that the novelist ought to express his own opinion on the things of this world," said Flaubert, "he can communicate it, but I do not like him to say it." "A novel," said Hardy more simply, "is an impression, not an argument."

To many people who hope to write novels, this will be an unwelcome reminder. But it is a necessary one. You should scrutinise your own motives, looking with suspicion and alarm upon any directly informative or didactic element that they may contain. In so far as you are motivated by urges of this sort, you are embarking upon a difficult and dangerous project.

The trouble isn't that your lecture is likely to be a bad one. It may well be first-class; but for the novel-reader, even so, it will usually be a distraction and an irrelevance. Things may even work out the other way round : you may offer us so deep and fascinating a lecture that we find ourselves distracted and bored by the purely fictional elements in your book. These characters and their words and their deeds may (we feel) be all very well; but why do they have to keep on crashing and interrupting into the room, while we and the author are enjoying a most fruitful philosophical discussion? A response of this kind, to the work of some good lecturer who has forcibly made himself into a bad novelist, is no rare thing.

This does not mean, of course, that definite strong opinions are fatal to the novelist. But they do need to be kept in their place. They can usefully colour a novelist's whole manner of thinking and writing, they can give edge and power to his observation and his responses. That is to say, they can serve the purposes of the novel. But if the novel tries to serve *their* purposes, it will very commonly die in the attempt.

Duly sacrificed upon the altar of pure irresponsible fiction, your opinions and your public or philosophical urgencies can rise again in greater power. *Uncle Tom's Cabin* succeeded in modifying the American awareness of slavery, and therefore the fact and the outcome of the Civil War, and therefore the subsequent nature of American society and the whole course of subsequent history : in these large affairs, its moral lesson played a small but definite part. But it did this only by being a good story first of all.

If your novel has some large purpose or message beyond itself, it must usually be content to achieve the purpose and convey the message indirectly. Angus Wilson makes the point well, speaking of the novelist's task "of disseminating the moral proposition so completely in a mass of living experience that it is never directly sensed as you read but only apprehended at the end as a result of the life you (the reader) have shared in the book". So apprehended in the reader's mind, and deeply, your moral proposition —or whatever else might have tempted you to lecture—will get across far more effectively than if you had forced it upon us by direct bludgeoning statement and insistence.

That young man at the party was wasting his breath : his knowledge and wisdom, so tellingly put forth, will be lost to the world. If only for this reason, he should have been more tactful.

(ii) *"Don't be rude."* **On** certain occasions and in some kinds of company, the conventions permit things to be said that are, on the surface, grossly insulting. In the course of one kind of alcoholic argument, you can call the other man a stupid bastard and not get your nose punched : at one stage in an agreeably-developing relationship, you can enchant the young lady by calling her a frightful old bag. But care is needed; and that young man from the outback should play this game cautiously or not at all.

The novelist should not insult his readers. He is hardly able to insult them personally, since he doesn't know who they are; and general abuse, directed at the whole human race or at some particular group, will seldom give offence. However precisely the cap fits him, each reader will assume that your vituperation is directed at other people, and he won't mind in the least. From Beachcomber back to Swift and earlier, abuse and denunciation of the public has always been a good selling line.

But you insult any man seriously if you treat him as a fool; and in this respect, many inexperienced novelists act imprudently and arouse resentment.

There are many different kinds of novel, and they are aimed at readers differing widely in their intelligence, their cultural level. But whatever readership you have in mind, make allowance for the fact that most people are reasonably quick on the uptake and can often take a hint. Don't spell everything out for us in words of one syllable : don't talk down to us : don't make the same point again and again, as though we were too slow-witted to take it in the first time. Give us the credit for a little alacrity of mind : don't have the manner of a weary teacher who's dealing with mentally defective children.

This applies to the substance of what your novel says, as well as to the tone of voice in which you say it. A great many novelists labour the obvious, cumbrously informing us of something that we knew already. There's no need to tell us that the world contains much evil; or that bloody-minded self-assertion commonly bears fruit in a loveless and unhappy life; or that large concentrations of money or power in the hands of money-lovers or power-lovers are seldom to be wholly trusted; or that business and the dollar make poor gods. A bad novel will often depend far too simply upon a statement of some such undoubtable truth : it will be put forward, not as a datum, a familiar part of experience that can be studied fruitfully, but rather as an exciting new discovery on the part of the brainy author, needing to be communicated to us doltish readers. Such treatment hurts our feelings.

Don't labour the obvious. You may assume that your readers know quite as much about life as you do : it is your task to heighten their perceptions, their awareness—not to enlighten their ignorance.

(iii) *"Don't show off."* Your general sense of superiority to the common herd is, of course, thoroughly justified; but if you display it too frankly, your fellow-guests won't always be pleased.

Handled properly, a display of sophistication can flatter the reader : you can make him feel that he's taking part in a private and privileged dialogue between exalted equals. Allusions and quotations, of just the correct difficulty, can have this effect : a somewhat dated and middlebrow version of the technique can be studied in the detective stories of Dorothy Sayers. You can also use private in-jokes, so long as they are not really 'in', really secret.

But there is great rudeness, great arrogance in the behaviour of the party-guest who talks on the assumption that everybody knows and cares about his petty circle of friends and their private jokes : with the implication that if you *don't* know and care about this fascinating in-group, you must be some kind of comic outsider and peasant. People don't like being made to feel small and outside; and there's always the possibility that your in-world may be smaller, shabbier, less fascinating than you suppose.

Be careful about showing off. You may be no end of a smart urbane sophisticate : you may have travelled, and wonderfully, not in the package-tour style of the humble; you may have a splendid *haut-école* grand-cooking-and-eating-and-wining thing: you may know all about wave-mechanics or Hindu philosophy. Deploy your greatness tactfully, and you may well charm us dim suburbanites : deploy it crudely, and you may well become a terrible bore.

(iv) *"Have a little consideration for others."* This is indeed a fundamental rule of social morality and social prudence. Our gauche young man can easily enjoy that party thoroughly, but at other people's expense : if so, he won't be asked again. He should have thought of others, seeking to make the whole occasion an enjoyable one for all concerned.

The novelist can rightly attend to his own pleasure in writing: the book that was fun to write is quite often fun to read. But this is a limited and somewhat dangerous principle : it cannot always be depended upon. The novelist should therefore remember that there are two parties to the transaction, himself and the reader, and that their interests will not necessarily coincide at every point; also, that if he hopes to be published, the reader must be put first. The writing of your novel may have been an unspeakable joy and relief to yourself; but unless it's likely to please other people as well, the publisher will look upon it with suspicion.

Beware, therefore, of a certain all-but-universal habit of the present-day mind, according to which 'art' is primarily self-expression. By all means express yourself, and other things as well: let your novel be authentically your own: let it emerge from your own life, your own experience, as seen in full integrity. But don't suppose that this will be enough.

A great many poets, when talking about their art, drop instinctively and sub-consciously into the use of obstetrical and even lavatorial imagery. To them, a poem is something that will make them uncomfortable until they've got it out. This is fair enough: people are entitled to attend to their own comfort. But these poets also seem to assume, and rashly, that when they have externalised onto paper the thing that was troubling them, the outcome should also and automatically be interesting to other people. They therefore come to feel a sense of grievance if people don't want to read their poems.

This is an unrealistic way of thinking: there's no necessary or obvious connection between relieving oneself and pleasing other people. The idea that there is such a connection, and that 'art' can realistically be equated with self-expression, has done any amount of harm, generating endless sterilities and follies and hypocrisies. Don't think on these lines. The publisher's reader is continually afflicted with masturbatory novels, obviously successful as self-expression or self-relief, wholly irrelevant to the needs and desires and pleasures of any other party but the writer. Think of others if you want to be published.

The self-centred and inconsiderate novelist often betrays himself by needless obscurity: he makes things unnecessarily hard for his readers, imposing upon them grievous burdens of de-coding and puzzling out, and offering them no sufficient reward for their exertions. He loses their goodwill at an early stage, and his company won't be sought in future.

The complexity of the question needs to be recognised. Not all obscurity is unjustified : not every good novel can be instantly understood and appreciated in full by an idle and inattentive reader of limited intelligence. And the concept of 'obscurity' is a relative one : your novel may well be impenetrably dark to some readers, luminous and lucid to others. It is entirely legitimate for the novelist to embark upon a project that will necessarily be obscure in one way or another, involving hard work on the reader's part. There are large tracts of human experience that cannot be handled truthfully on simple and obvious lines; and quite apart from this, there is a positive pleasure in the solving of puzzles and the answering of riddles. Absolute simplicity, direct-ness, and clarity in the conduct of narrative can be a great merit in the novelist, and it calls for a kind of skill that you should certainly have at your disposal, for use when required. But for many perfectly sound projects, quite different merits are appro-priate.

If your readers are going to be made to work, however, they must be rewarded for their exertions. Obscurity is often the necessary condition of high achievement : but you should regard it as being a bad thing in itself, to be tolerated reluctantly in a good cause, never to be indulged for its own sake.

Many bad novelists do appear to indulge it for its own sake : they seem to generate riddling complexities at random, hoping thereby to cloak the naked poverty of their work with outer garments of esoteric sophistication. Literary awareness, con-centrating chiefly upon the eccentricities of genius, has led them to associate the twentieth-century novel with various kinds of darkness and difficulty : made disproportionately nervous by minority-fashion, they strain anxiously towards the anti-novel, or the un-novel, or the levon, and they look down in superior contempt upon mere comprehensible narrative. Their chief aspiration is towards a novel that will baffle Aunt Edna completely, and will in fact not be recognisable as a novel at all, not in her presbyopic eyes.

Perhaps this is a caricature : perhaps few novelists, or none at all, are motivated by a snobbery so very childish. But the publisher's reader, sighing heavily over another four hundred pages of clever impenetrable bosh, must be forgiven for the prejudices born of long experience. To him, it seems quite apparent that such snobberies do prevail, and widely, and only occasionally to any useful purpose.

Think of others. It is your prime task to please people; and while you can reasonably ask them to be intelligent and attentive, and often to respond in complex and cerebral fashion, you must not set needless obstacles in the path of their enjoyment. Let your novel be as lucid, as considerate as its nature permits. Don't blind us with science : don't baffle us with your monstrous cleverness. If you do, we'll only turn away and talk to somebody else.

(v) *"Don't outstay your welcome."* Intoxicated by the gaiety of the occasion and the sound of his own voice, as well as by the refreshment provided, that young party-guest may still be there—irremoveably—when the others have all roared off into the night, when his hostess starts to yawn and fidget and tidy up the mess, even when his host flings back the curtains to admit the rosy-fingered dawn. He makes this mistake in a spirit of pure happiness and goodwill : he won't be forgiven easily.

There can indeed be some difficulty in this question of when to go. But the practical rule is simple and obvious : when in doubt, go too early rather than too late. Make other people wish that they'd seen more of you, not less of you : then you may be asked again, even if your too-early departure gave mild offence at the time. If you become known as a guest who outstays his welcome, it will ruin your social prospects.

It has to be admitted that the publisher's reader is prejudiced in favour of short books : his heart warms towards the author whose writing is economical and brief, the one who says what he has to say and then goes. There's usually a big pile of type-scripts awaiting the reader's attention; and since he's commonly paid by the individual book, without reference to its length, a very long novel will constitute a relatively ill-paid and therefore an unwelcome task.

By harsh self-discipline, he endeavours to overcome this prejudice. Indulged, it will distort his judgment. Brevity is not always a virtue: for some novels, for some purposes of the novel in general, mere length is desirable. "The object of a story is to be long, to fill up hours," said Stevenson. "You can't get a cup of tea large enough or a book long enough to suit me," said C. S. Lewis, according to Walter Hooper: who adds "And he meant it for at that moment I was pouring his tea into a very large Cornish-ware cup and he was reading *Bleak House*."

Ideally speaking, every novel has its own due and proper length, and towards this the novelist gropes in the course of his writing, reaching (let us hope) more or less the correct answer. There's always a right moment for leaving the party, and it may come early or late. You certainly don't want the word 'padding' to occur in the reader's report; you don't want it to be said that your novel dragged on and on miserably, or that like some after-dinner speakers, you couldn't think how to stop. On the other hand, a skimped, bare, hurried novel offers poor thin nourishment to the reader. You have to strike the balance that's appropriate in this particular case.

But if in doubt, go early; and not only for the sake of relieving the burden upon the publisher's reader. To the aspiring novelist, needless prolixity is (in general) a far greater danger than excessive curtness. For every novel that would be healthier if it put on a little more weight, there are ten that need to sweat off some fat. Among our party-rules, this might be included: *"Don't talk too much."*

Various factors are involved here, not all of them purely literary. The notorious rush of life, in what's supposed to be a leisured society, means that there's now rather less demand for the very long novel than there was in Dickens's time, or even in

Stevenson's: not all of us need our hours to be filled up, not all of us have time or desire for those enormous cups of tea. In general, with exceptions, we prefer sharper drinks in smaller containers.

The huge novel, all lavish and profuse and multiple, can indeed still be written and sold. But the aspiring novelist, whose talent is perhaps marginal and certainly not established yet, will usually be well advised to aim at something more compact. Other things being equal, he will then have a better chance of publication. Commercially speaking, any first novel is a gamble; and the longer it is, the more rash the gamble will be, the less attractive to the prudent business-man who runs that publishing office. Typesetting is a very expensive process; paper might seem to be a cheap commodity, but it's surprisingly expensive when bought by the ton; machining and binding grow more complicated and expensive as a book grows longer. A very long novel represents a bigger investment on the publisher's side; its price will be higher, and it will therefore be harder to sell. For the publisher's representative, it's already quite difficult enough to persuade some bookseller—struggling, disillusioned, and over-stocked already—that he ought to order this new novel by an unheard-of name : don't make the task harder.

If you have several novels in mind, one of them immensely long and the others more compact, defer the long one until your established name can help to justify the cost of producing it. Be modest, at first, in the literary or social burdens that you inflict upon other people. The day will come when your host and hostess *want* you to stay behind when the other guests have gone, talking the whole night away in your own lovely and luminous fashion. But don't rush things.

The thoughtful reader of this book will be able to work out further rules for himself, enriching his concept of well-mannered writing by his experience of social behaviour. When some foolish character manages to alienate his company unintentionally, let the episode be considered, let a literary parallel be sought : very often a moral can be deduced, useful to the novelist who hopes to please.

But each man lives and writes within his own compartment of a very complex society, and concepts of acceptable behaviour vary widely. Conduct that would be perfectly correct at an embassy reception might seem intolerable in a candle-lit *discothèque*; and *vice*, of course, *versa*. Novels vary in the same way. Let your literary manners be precisely adapted to the present task and the desired readership. Perfect upper-class mandarin elegance will often be a gross and loutish mistake.

But whatever your project and your company may be, good manners will always dictate a close attention to the detailed problems of writing, to the choice of words and the design of sentences, to what some people call 'style'. You must write well.

'Good writing' appears to be a somewhat elusive concept: extraordinary ideas are entertained about it. It must therefore be declared roundly that only one single meaning can usefully be attributed to that phrase. 'Good writing' is writing that does precisely the work that's currently being asked of it: that and nothing else. All expressions of stylistic praise or blame are therefore relative: you must not say, in any absolute fashion, that it's either good or bad for your writing to be economical, or wild, or verbose, or sentimental, or tense, or pedantic, or slangy, or extravagant. It all depends upon the task and the occasion.

But language is always a precision tool; and if you want your novel to be readable, you must handle it with precision. This applies with particular force to your detailed choice of words. As languages go, English has a very large vocabulary: it is privileged to draw upon two quite separate verbal stockpots, one being Germanic in origin and the other Latin, where most languages have to make do with one. These are further supplemented by a surprising variety of other resources, chiefly garnered in the ramshackle processes of trade and Empire. It follows that in handling the English language, one often comes across a pair or a group of words that mean *more or less* the same thing: near-synonyms abound in English.

In this situation, there is a great profit and great danger. Words that are approximately synonymous often differ very sharply and usefully in their associations, their emotional overtones, their precise meanings. A 'foe' is not quite the same thing as an 'enemy'; you 'fall' in a straight line, but 'tumble' with a rotary motion; it's more forgiveable if you call a man 'a pig' than if you call him 'a swine'. By a careful choice of the exact word, from several alternatives, the writer of English can therefore suggest a fullness and precision of meaning that could otherwise only be conveyed by circumlocution or by grammatical devices. The Frenchman, with his smaller vocabulary, must first analyse and then state meanings that we can—more economically—suggest: a necessity which may be responsible for the curious idea that the French are a notably logical race. This means also that English is an outstandingly useful language for poetry.

Unfortunately, it also means that English offers unparalleled scope for inaccurate and mushy writing. It's a splendid language for talking nonsense in, or for generating vague verbal fog: it's the ideal language for a politician, it offers wonderful scope for the avoidance of precise and responsible thinking. For the novelist, it's dangerous. As he proceeds, pen in hand, he comes up against an endless series of minute tactical problems involving the choice of words. And in a great many such cases, there will be several words available, each one of them able to meet the necessity of the moment in a rough approximate sort of way. One of them will be the right word: the rest will be slightly, subtly wrong. But the writer who's careless or insensitive will use the first one that comes to mind, overlooking the fact that it isn't exactly the one he needs: it does the job after a fashion, and he lets it go at that. In a single case, little damage will be done; but the cumulative effect will be disastrous, suggesting a photograph that's badly out of focus. The trouble is not that writing of this off-target kind breaks the rules and offends the pundits: it simply doesn't work properly, it's lame. The author never quite succeeds in saying what he had in mind : at every point, he says something subtly different instead. He fails to communicate : even the lowbrow reader, not consciously fastidious about language, will find the book a bore.

Countless novels fail and are damned because of the prevalence within them of the *mot injuste,* the slightly and infuriatingly wrong word. The publisher's reader goes mad with frustration while reading them : he wants to do some savage amending, but he isn't allowed to mark the typescript.

Let the aspiring novelist beware. He does not always need a very large vocabulary, and he should usually be very careful indeed about fancy talk, exhumed archaisms, inkhorn terms, and ostentatious cleverness of vocabulary in general. But he does need to use words accurately.

To put the matter at the lowest : he should never use any word unless he's quite sure of its meaning. This is ambiguous counsel, of course : the dictionary will often suggest one meaning and popular usage another. The novelist can often follow popular usage quite safely, doing things that would have outraged the English master at his school : but at least he should know what he's doing, he should be aware of changing and alternative meanings. He should know, for example, that 'an internecine war' is an exceptionally bloody and murderous war, not necessarily a war of the civil or fratricidal kind; he should know that you're 'oblivious' of something when you've forgotten it, not when you're just unaware of it; he should know the difference between 'infer' and 'imply'. A novel is not a work of scholarship or pedantry, and for some purposes its language can often be wildly colloquial and 'incorrect', especially and obviously in connection with dialogue : if Harry Mubble is a slab-carrier in a grimy glue-mill, don't make him talk like Harold Nicolson. But no kind of ignorance about words and their functioning is likely to be really helpful to the novelist.

Be in love with words, in all their rich and awkward individuality.

Be in love also with sentences : with their structures and

shapes and rhythms and resonances. Cultivate an ear for their sound.

When you write them, let them at least be clear. Even if you wish to suggest darkness, confusion, and torrential nonsense, you must do it with clarity. Distinguish the writing itself from the effect given: they aren't the same thing. Dark, confused, torrential, nonsensical writing will not achieve even that purpose.

Don't oblige the publisher's reader to read each sentence several times over, trying with furrowed brow to work out whatever it was that this wretched author was trying to say. Even in your own interest, have more courtesy, than that, more consideration.

In this connection, the time-honoured rule is still useful: write by mouth and ear, not by eye. Before you put pen to paper, let every sentence be formulated in your mind and then mouthed over experimentally: listen to it, and don't write it down until you're quite sure that it *sounds* right. This rehearsal, this preliminary mouthing-over should be done aloud if possible; and so should your subsequent corrective reading-over of every passage, every paragraph. The family may quite possibly raise their eyebrows when they hear you, muttering and gibbering to yourself over there in your corner. Then seek solitude for your writing, if circumstances permit: otherwise, ignore the family. Their doubts of your sanity are of small account, compared with the necessity for your writing to please the ear, and to be produced therefore by a mouth-and-ear technique. You are practising an art that's essentially a sound-thing, only a few steps removed—even now—from the vocal and aural art of the epic singer, the bard of ancient days: keep in touch with your origins. That old bearded character would have had things flung at him—chewed hambones, empty mead-flagons—if he inflicted upon the assembled warrior-company such chaotic jaw-breaking chokepear sentences as are now inflicted daily upon the publisher's reader.

Be gentle, be good-mannered. I've never done you any harm.

CHAPTER EIGHT

A MIRROR UP TO NATURE?

YOUR NOVEL IS, of course, a pack of lies from start to finish; and not for one single moment is anyone who reads it going to imagine otherwise. "No art produces illusion," said Stevenson; "in the theatre we never forget that we are in the theatre."

On the other hand, your novel has to carry conviction: it needs to foster, or at the very least it must not obstruct, what Coleridge called "that willing suspension of disbelief for the moment, which constitutes poetic faith". In some sense of the word, the novelist therefore has a duty of 'realism': his work must ring true, its falsehood must not be apparent. If he fails in this respect, he fails seriously: words like 'unconvincing' and 'implausible' are very destructive when they occur in a reader's report.

But this is a complex question: the 'realism' needed by a novel stands in no simple relationship to the vague shimmering phantasmagoria that we call 'real life'. A science-fantasy or a fairy-tale can be completely realistic or convincing in the required sense, suspending our disbelief absolutely, though the events portrayed may be not merely impossible in the world of experience but entirely nonsensical as well, quite incapable of taking place in any conceivable universe. Wells's *Time Machine* is a case in point. How uncritically we swallow the concept of the 'Time Traveller', pedalling down the centuries on that glittering quasi-bicycle of his, with its quartz rods, and occasionally jamming on the brakes and pausing for a few moments to see what has happened to the world! We 'believe' in him completely; and yet, when we look at it in cold blood, we feel a strong suspicion that the whole idea is not merely a technical impossibility but a logical absurdity as well. It doesn't seem to mean a thing: but Wells has dexterously and most fruitfully concealed the fact from us. Conversely, the pursuit of 'realism' —in some straight documentary sense of that word—often leads the unskilled novelist into the portrayal of a world that carries no conviction at all, even though all the characters and all the happenings in it are entirely possible and indeed entirely familiar.

The skilled liar can fool anybody. On the other hand, there are some people whose manner causes them to be distrusted and disbelieved, even when they are speaking the truth.

The story-teller has never needed to worry very much about physical possibility. Many of us can recognise a logical absurdity when it is brought to our attention; but even in an age of science, men simply do not know the limits of what can and what cannot happen in the world of beings and objects. It is sometimes supposed that 'modern science' has positively disproved the existence of (say) leprechauns and werewolves and unicorns; but no such claim will be made by anybody who knows the nature and limitations of scientific method. We still live in a universe alien and unexplored, full of barely credible things—things alien to the daily habit of our mind; and to the reader of fiction, surprises and marvels of all kinds will seem sufficiently plausible, in the required sense, if they're put across in the right way.

Plausibility will often be helped by the trappings of authority, if this is of a kind that we normally respect. Professor Tolkien's heroic romance *The Lord of the Rings* is staged in a wholly imagined world, parallel to our own but independent of it; and it carries enormous conviction, partly because the wise author has underpinned his vast exercise in self-consistent imaginative creation with a *trompe l'oeil* structure of literary and historical scholarship, with dates and footnotes and every kind of lecture-room dullness. A rather similar method lends frightening plausibility to the ghost stories of M. R. James. We all respect scholarship, we are well aware that professors know more than we do : if we are to believe in unbelievable countries of the universe or of the mind, their kind of sober reassurance will help us along.

The same goes, more dramatically, for science. The vast and shadowy structure that we call 'modern science' is, for us, the exact equivalent of fairyland—another world, touching our own, explored piecemeal by intrepid adventurers but known as a whole to no man : a world not understood, full of promise and terror : a world in which anything can happen, so that we need to go carefully, our nerves tingling. By plausibly invoking this world and its powers, the novelist can suspend our disbelief most wonderfully, persuading us of marvels, telling us the oldest of fairy-tales once again. His gallant knight in armour will, perhaps, have become a Space-Lieutenant in a natty green uniform, wielding a nucleonic blaster rather than a trusty sword; the damsel in distress will presumably wear those curious sprayed-on tights that tend to be always dropping off one shoulder; the dragon will have become a five-dimensional jellyfish. But in most senses, it will be the same story.

The 'science' in science-fiction serves only to convey us plausibly into a world of unfamiliar and unexpected happenings. For a primitive or peasant readership, such a world could be staged in the unknown and frightening depths of the adjacent forest; for a nineteenth-century readership, it could be staged in the yet unexplored jungles of Africa or the distant Amazon. But we know those jungles and forests, or we think we do; we suspect that aerial photography would have discovered Professor Challenger's lost world by now, and we feel quite sure that there are no trolls and hobgoblins and undefinable presences in Epping Forest. For us, therefore, the unchanging land of terrors and marvels has to be staged on some distant world or in some unprecedented relationship to space and time. The science, the technology can make this seem plausible; and it is nearly always rash for the inexperienced novelist to give it any other function.

Such considerations might perhaps seem relevant only to the novelist who specialises in fantasy. None the less, the whole question of 'realism' can usefully be approached from this angle: our pedestrian daily routines, the realistic novelist's raw materials, come closer to wild fantasy or improbability than we commonly suppose.

Life as a whole is most unlikely, and so is every item within it. Considered antecedently and in statistical terms, your own existence is grossly improbable. It wasn't at all likely that those two particular people, your parents, should meet and marry; or that they should make love on that particular occasion; or that the millions-to-one lottery of conception should have thrown up this particular end-product. Yet here, surprisingly, you are.

Everything that happens is arbitrary, an extraordinary coincidence. We all feel it as an uncanny coincidence if well-shuffled cards are dealt to four people, and if each player then finds his hand to comprise a single suit, perfect and in the right order. Witnessing this, we would feel almost frightened, as though a devil or the Holy Ghost had intervened: we would desperately *need* to believe that the cards had been fiddled and arranged by somebody. But considered antecedently, that disposition of the cards is no more and no less unlikely than any other.

Habit, and a certain torpor of the mind, conceal from us the fact that every actual happening has that gross and extreme improbability which—in some systems of physics—means something that can't be distinguished from scientific impossibility. All things are unique and barely credible: their existence is arbitrary and something of a marvel.

If the novelist is imaginatively aware of this, he will make a sound approach to the task of being 'realistic'. He deals in the concrete: he never says "Things of this kind tend to happen", but always "This particular thing *did* happen". He must recognise the improbability and assert the fact.

From the beginning of time, men have been bothered by the paradox of free-will and destiny. We *know* that we make free choices and that the future is undecided: none the less, after the event, we recognise fate, we see that it *had* to happen that way.

The novel's ultimate realism lies in its fidelity to this paradox, to this tension: every development, every happening within the story must be unpredictable before it happens, and must also appear—*after* it happens—to have been inevitable from the start. In this respect always, and occasionally in no other respect at all, a novel needs to be 'true to life'.

In various more pedestrian senses, the novelist must of course pursue truth or 'realism'. His story must not clash grossly with anything that lies within our certain knowledge, and especially with our knowledge of human nature. We don't know what the ultimate possibilities of the universe are, but we do know a little about how people actually behave. You can easily make us believe that you saw a ghost last night, or that there are men nine miles high upon Jupiter, despite screams of scientific protest; but you will never make us believe that when Queen Victoria first asked Mr Gladstone to form a ministry, he slapped her on the back and offered her a cigar and told her a dirty story. The example is Chesterton's, and he was right: no amount of first-hand contemporary documentation could make such a story seem even faintly plausible. And yet it suggests no violation of any law of nature: in a sense, it is entirely possible.

We can believe the impossible far more easily than the psychologically improbable.

Your novel will be realistic, in the required sense, if it is true to human nature and human experience: when some novel fails grossly in plausibility, one's usual diagnosis is that the author leads too solitary and withdrawn a life. He ought to get around a little more; he ought to attend more observantly to the human race.

He must, of course, take care not to distract and irritate us by manifest error in known matters: in so far as his novel has factual reference, his facts must be right. He should not let the full moon hang low in the west at sunset; he should not represent his coal-miners as lighting cheerful campfires in those explosive underground corridors. And many a novel will depend for a major part of its effect upon a full documentation of some authentic and specialised mode of existence: in such a case, and often in connection with the historical novel, the author will have a good deal of homework and research to do, and he must do it properly.

None the less, the concept of 'realism' can be taken too seriously and too literally: it can conceal from the novelist the fact that he is proposing to practise a highly-stylised and conventional art-form. He may then achieve the realism·and neglect the art, so that his book comes to resemble a newspaper photograph, and a dull one, rather than a live painting, a news item rather than a poem.

He has something more arbitrary and complex than that to achieve, something less flat and rational. Over-familiarity with the idea of 'the novel' should not make him suppose that it is an obvious and straightforward idea. It is not. It took many centuries for the European mind to become accustomed to the idea that sustained prose fiction might be a legitimate or even a possible thing; and in its eighteenth-century beginnings, the modern novel commonly wore some pretence, some contrived machinery of being factual. It dressed itself up as a journal or a set of letters, such as might quite conceivably be discovered in somebody's drawer. If some literal-minded person were to ask how the manuscript of *Pamela* or *Clarissa Harlowe* had originated, an untrue but plausible answer would be available.

But the modern novel—on the face of it—purports to be something which it cannot possibly be in fact. If told in the first person, it supposes in the narrator a memory impossibly long and detailed and precise; if told in the third person, it supposes a kind and degree of knowledge—including the knowledge of other people's minds in their secret operation—which nobody has in fact. The falsehood of the modern novel is glaringly obvious: by convention, we ignore it.

The novel-convention is a pretence that we put on, a game that we play, in connection with the limitations of human knowledge and the consequent painful mystery of human existence. Forster suggests that a great deal of the novel's attraction lies in this fact. We are defeated, he says, by the unknowability of real people; "And that is why novels, even when they are about wicked people, can solace us: they suggest a more comprehensible and thus a more manageable human race, they give us the illusion of perspicacity and power."

An illusion it is indeed: if the reader suddenly took it into his head to address the novelist in his human and private capacity, and ask "But how do you *know* all this?", the novelist would have no beginning of a positive reply. Truthfully but lamely, he would have to admit that he had made it up; and the illusion, the attraction would collapse at once.

If a novel is to carry conviction, it is one of the novelist's prime tasks to distract and hold the reader's attention so decisively that this fatal question is never allowed to arise. If it does arise, all is lost. The inexperienced novelist therefore needs to be especially careful when he handles any subject-matter that, by reason of its obvious unknowability, tends to raise that question in an acute and urgent way.

There is an old familiar anecdote about a man who fell asleep in church and dreamt that he was an aristocrat at the time of the French Revolution and was about to be guillotined. The lever was pulled, the knife started to fall; and at that moment, his wife noticed that he was asleep and tapped him sharply on the back of the neck with her fan in order to wake him up. The fan-tap became the blade-cut, and the man died at once from heart failure.

Some people can hear that story and not notice anything wrong with it: but most will observe that it strains the convention of narrative too far. The aspiring novelist will probably never make quite so gross a mistake as that; but he should remember the anecdote and take warning from it. He is a confidence-man pitching a most implausible yarn, a salesman pushing a manifestly phoney product: the victim must not be given any chance to ask awkward questions. "The natural habit of any good and critical reader," says Angus Wilson, "is to disbelieve what you are telling him and try to escape out of the world you are picturing." You have to give him the treatment, you have to bring him under control.

You can easily be distracted from this necessity if you take the word 'realism' too literally, and then proceed as though your main task was the precise transcription of actual experience. It is not so : you are concerned with an art-form that is not realistic, or even representational at all, except in a very limited way. A novel is an arrangement, a pattern, designed so as to have a certain effect upon the reader and evoke a certain response from him : it resembles a semi-abstract painting, of the kind that includes representational elements, far more closely than it resembles a photograph.

Art is not like life : despite Hamlet's tiresome half-truth, it does not function usefully by holding a mirror up to nature, unless we are to imagine a mirror that can do some very elaborate selection and distortion and re-arrangement. Virginia Woolf points out that life, as experienced, is not in the least like a well-tailored novel : it is "a luminous halo, a semi-transparent envelope surrounding us from the beginning of consciousness to the end". Many modern novels have tried to capture and record this fact, adapting their technique accordingly. At their best they have approximated to the condition of poetry, so that it ceases to be useful to call them 'novels' at all; and while they have rightly attracted much critical attention, they tend to have only a specialised kind of appeal. The story-teller's art is perennially needed by humanity, but it has limitations : it cannot do all things.

To the novelist, 'real life' is not a subject to be photographed: it is a kind of storehouse or quarry, from which he can select the elements that he needs in order to construct the special pattern that interests him at the moment. The pattern itself will seldom be provided by real life. This does contain certain elements of new beginning, of climax, of ending and the settling of questions; but these occur in faint and mixed versions, and for the novelist's purposes they need to be picked out, isolated, intensified, and arranged in highly artificial fashion, so as to constitute a pleasure-giving pattern of experience for the reader. "As regards plot," says Ivy Compton-Burnett, "I find real life no help at all. Real life seems to have no plot. And as I think a plot desirable and almost necessary, I have this extra grudge against life." "Life is amorphous, art is formal," says Françoise Sagan.

Many novels fail on these lines: their writers transcribed experience with total fidelity and total dullness. In such a case, the reader will be tempted to explode with impatience at around the eightieth page. "Yes, yes, yes; but why am I being *told* all this?"

Once again, an unanswerable question; once again, the novelist must prevent it from being asked, and this will involve him in very careful selectivity. From the proposition "This actually happens in real life" he must never make the direct inference "This can be usefully put into my novel". It doesn't follow: factual realism is only part of the game. "There are scenes in life that cannot be written, even if they can be proved to have happened," said George Moore. "It does not seem to me to be enough to say of any description that it is the exact truth," said Dickens: "the exact truth must be there; but the merit of art in the narrator is the manner of stating the truth."

One occasionally meets a writer who claims that his novel *must* be a good one, since everything in it actually happened, to his own certain knowledge. His fallacy is total.

Another danger can arise, in certain circumstances, if you take the concept of 'realism' too seriously: you may falsify your novel by an irrelevant, one-sided, and indeed unrealistic concentration upon the ugly side of things.

This danger arises directly from the overtones of meaning that the word 'realism' and its derivatives have recently come to possess. During the last hundred years or so, the development of popular psychology has caused us all to become acutely aware that we belong to a self-deceiving race. Human beings fool themselves; they tend to ignore whatever perplexes or distresses them, and to pretend that it doesn't exist. In various degrees, most of us do have this tendency to look upon life through rose-tinted spectacles; and it can truly be said that certain novelists present a sweet and sentimentalised view of things, a comfortable world of illusion, into which their readers can retreat in a spirit of escapism.

To many stern people, this seems highly reprehensible; and it is widely felt, therefore, that the novelist and his readers are acting in a praiseworthy fashion if the whole exercise is made to have an unflinchingly 'realistic' character—if our noses are rubbed in the harsh realities, the ugly truths all faced, the sweet illusions all mocked and rejected, with no concessions made at all to any kind of escapism, or even to any kind of prudery or reticence. This (it is felt) will be the policy of the *honest* novelist: any alternative policy will involve him in hypocrisy, and his book will be fictitious in a most improper sense.

There is obviously some truth here. It is truth, however, of a moral rather than a strictly literary variety : if some critic urges us to be—in this sense—'realistic', he is trespassing upon ground that more properly belongs to the preacher or the moral philosopher.

But the whole truth is not of this kind. If human beings have a tendency to indulge in prettified sentimental illusion, they also have a converse tendency to wallow with great enjoyment in gloom and squalor. This also can be a form of self-indulgence and even of self-deception : the 'realism' that is urged upon us as a stern moral duty often turns out in practice to be a luscious orgy and a flight from fact. Some people are so determinedly 'realistic' that they cannot bear to admit the existence of anything nice.

Each of these two opposed tendencies is partially realistic in fact : each corresponds to a mood that most of us have for part of the time, and some of us for most of the time. There are days upon which it seems that God's in his heaven and all's right with the world. Upon such days, we look with admiration upon wise men and beautiful women, we see hope and promise everywhere, we believe in happy endings. Then, in another mood on another day, we see humanity as a writhing swarm of tortured maggots, blind, absurd, suffering pointlessly in a cold and alien universe : all things seem horrifying and mad. Both moods, both visions have their validity, their limited and partial truth : most of us are familiar with each of them, though any individual may tend—by reason of his psychology, or his glands, or the circumstances of his life—to concentrate upon the one or the other. Each makes perfectly valid subject-matter for the novelist : each can be, in its distinctive way, highly enjoyable.

But it is a mistake to suppose that one is overwhelmingly more true than the other, and (especially) that 'realism' dictates a systematic concentration upon the seamy side and the gloomy view. Life, as we actually experience it, is a very mixed affair, an inextricable tangle of good and bad, of nice and nasty. We are certainly open to the charge of sentimentality if we see every-thing *couleur de rose;* but we are open to exactly the same charge if we see everything *couleur de merde.*

The particular self-pitying sentimentality of our age means that for every novelist who commits the first offence, there are ten who commit the second. In either case, the publisher's reader is aware of falsification. Let your novel express any view of things that seems authentic to yourself. But don't let your own perceptions and responses be falsified; don't be intimidated by 'the spirit of the age'—or by any similar hobgoblin—into either kind of sentimentality. Try to be realistic about the mixed and tolerable character that life usually has.

The novels handled by the publisher's reader include a great many which seem to have been written by dedicated counter-sentimentalists. Towards such writers, he comes to feel a certain impatience : he would like to get hold of them and shatter their illusions. In the name of realism, he would like to inform them that life has its wonderful aspects, that motives can be good and actions successful, that marriages can be happy and children a delight, that youth can be gentle and old age serene, and that laughter under the apple blossom can be just as 'real' as incest committed by maniacs in a dustbin in Huddersfield in the pouring rain.

The aspiring novelist may be reluctant to face these unpalatable facts. But he should : otherwise he will be in serious danger of telling lies and falsifying his art. "What one feels so hopelessly barren in declared pessimism," said Conrad, "is just its arrogance. It seems as if the discovery made by many men at various times that there is much evil in the world were a source of proud and unholy joy unto some of the modern writers. That frame of mind is not the proper one in which to approach seriously the art of fiction. It gives an author— goodness only knows why—an elated sense of his own superiority. And there is nothing more dangerous than such an elation to that absolute loyalty towards his feelings and sensations an author should keep hold of in his most exalted moments of creation."

The blind pursuit of 'realism', as the word tends to be understood nowadays, creates another danger for the aspiring novelist : it can tempt him towards ground which is undeniably attractive and undeniably real, but which has pitfalls in it, possibly unsuspected by himself.

As soon as the word is mentioned, one consequence is inevitable : somewhere at the back of our minds, sex will rear its ugly head. Sex has many diverse heads in point of fact— ugly, delightful, comic, holy, clinical, boring, frightening, and so forth—and it rears any or all of them on the slightest provocation. It is a mistake to suppose that 'realism' dictates an uncritical acquiescence in this tendency.

So far as social convention and legal restraints are concerned, the modern novel can be frank and 'realistic' about sex to a degree that is almost without precedent. Thackeray complained about the reticence of the nineteenth century : never since Fielding's day, he said, had it been possible for a novelist to portray the whole man. Now we have all Fielding's liberty, and a great deal more : it is no longer astonishing, it is no longer news when a novelist describes sexual activity with a fullness and detail that was previously confined to frankly pornographic writing. There has always been pornography, of course; but it has usually led a separate kind of existence, subterranean and furtive, quite distinct from the main stream of literature. If these two streams have now converged, the fact can—from certain points of view—be seen as a thoroughly good thing, enlarging the novelist's scope, enhancing the realism and relevance of his art, and blowing a little fresh air into regions of the mind that had previously festered with guilt and furtiveness and falsity.

With the moral, legal, and social aspects of the matter, this book will not be concerned. If your novel tends to be outspoken, with steamy couplings and an abundance of four-letter words and so forth, the publisher's reader will certainly mention the fact in his report. Different firms have their different and changing policies, and the book trade includes a great many people, having various attitudes to this question : if a book can—from *any* point of view—be called 'obscene', the publisher needs to have the fact drawn to his attention, as in the parallel matter of libel. He then has to make his own decision.

Strictly speaking, the publisher's reader is therefore not concerned with the question of obscenity. If you write a grossly pornographic novel, he will only be interested in the question of whether you've done it well or badly. In his personal capacity, he's case-hardened; he's already read any number of pornographic novels, some of them by madmen, and it's most unlikely that your particular handling of sex and its various friends and relations will either inflame or nauseate him. Like a priest in the confessional, he's heard it all before.

He is aware, however, that the pursuit of sexual frankness raises certain purely literary dangers for the inexperienced novelist; and in no spirit of prudery, he is therefore disposed to wag a cautionary finger.

In the first place, sexual frankness has now become something of a fashion and even something of a convention; and like every fashion and every convention, it threatens the artist with falsity. Imagine a society so totalitarian that every novelist was obliged to pay regular lip-service to the current party-line, as dictated by the ruffians in power. This requirement might do little harm to certain novels: to many or most, it would be disastrous. One would wish the novelist to have a free choice about his selection of subjects and his treatment of them.

But many novelists carry on as though a certain harping upon the physical aspects of sex has now become compulsory. One writer will discharge this obligation sparingly, feeling perhaps that the decencies and conventions will be observed sufficiently if there's just a distant decorous reference to a breast or a thigh on about every thirtieth page. Another, more loyal and docile, will feel that a convention so very authoritative and of-the-moment as this one deserves to be given a thorough-going and assiduous kind of observance: in the spirit of a moral rigorist, he will keep our noses always to the grindstone, our eyes always to the keyhole, remorselessly. In either case, there will often be an irrelevance, a falsity.

Don't put anything into your novel that doesn't really belong there, whatever the Thought-Police may threaten. And do your best to stomach this possibly unpalatable fact, that frank sexual description doesn't belong naturally in all novels, and will constitute an artistic blemish wherever it's dragged in by force.

The publisher's reader often encounters a novel that would have lived quite happily and at ease within the more reticent conventions of a few years ago, but has in fact been dirtied up, arbitrarily and awkwardly, in timid obedience to the fashion of this moment. He shakes his head sadly over such destructive cowardice.

In other cases, he feels—disapprovingly—that a novelist has used sex in order to cheat, to compel a response that he hasn't earned.

Somebody once put up a notice-board, desiring to draw the

public attention to whatever it was that he wanted to say or sell. At the top of the notice-board, he wrote in huge red letters the one word SEX; and under it, in much smaller letters, "Now that we have your undivided attention, may we point out that . . ." The message, of course, had nothing to do with sex; no doubt it was read closely and often, though in some disappointment.

People being what they are, sexy talk and sexy pictures will always attract attention immediately and powerfully : every advertiser knows this. The novelist can indeed rely upon the fact; but it is a pity, and it suggests a certain weakness in his other resources, if he *has* to rely upon it. If you focus attention upon sex—or, for that matter, upon violence, which is for many purposes the same thing—you will be able to cheat : you can then by-pass the strictly literary problem, assaulting your reader's nervous system crudely and directly, instead of appealing subtly to his imagination. "Politics in a work of literature," said Stendhal, "are like a pistol-shot in the middle of a concert, something loud and vulgar and yet a thing to which it is not possible to refuse one's attention." Now that we all care less about politics and more frankly about sex, this might be said with greater relevance of bedwork. Explode this in your novel, in every last sweaty detail, and attention will not be refused; but the weight, the crude neural impact of this item is very likely to shatter the fragile context. In practice, you will probably need to louden and vulgarise the whole of your concert so that your pistol-shot may seem to belong.

Literary skill of the highest kind will be able to resolve this difficulty. But the aspiring novelist should take warning. He is proposing to practise a very delicate art, depending upon texture and nuance and implication; he is a craftsman, handling the subtle tissues of language and experience. It's always open to him to drop this exacting and tedious discipline, and to grab the sledge-hammer of sex or violence, and crudely to bash the reader into submission. It will work : anybody can do it : the result will be saleable, just as a rude word shouted will always generate a stupefied silence and attention. But it will be an abdication of aesthetic responsibility. You can play subtler games than this; and if you want the publisher's reader to believe that you're a novelist with a future, don't be in too much of a visible hurry to take the easy way out.

If you do go in for sexual description, remember that it's hard to do well. Like certain other kinds of private experience, it strains the novel-convention: badly handled, it will very imprudently draw our attention to the fact that this narrative isn't what it claims to be. Thus, in the name of realism, credibility will be endangered.

Even in these permissive days, sexual behaviour is not normally catalogued in the subsequent speech or writing of either participant. Every piece of sexually descriptive narrative, where it's written in the third person or the first, has therefore a strained or improbable character: it is unlike anything that we normally say or write in daily life, and it is exceptionally vulnerable on that account to any semi-conscious questioning of its nature and *provenance*. Any such questioning will of course be anticipated and stalled in advance by the skilled novelist; but there's danger here for the lesser talent.

In general, the inexperienced novelist will act prudently if he only portrays things that are—in principle—knowable, either by observation and report or else by experience. In our society, sexual behaviour is not knowable, in any full degree, by either observation or personal report; and if the novelist relies upon remembered experience, he will be in danger of falsifying this very distinctive subject-matter. The involvement, the heightened experience of those passionate moments means that detached observation is impossible. In the event, the novelist very often contrives—but unintentionally—to suggest a loving couple who were never lost in that uncontrollable golden ecstasy at all: it will seem as though they were taking clinical notes all the time, studying and memorising their own actions and responses. To say the least of it, this will suggest a very odd specialised kind of love-making; and in practice, the ghosts of the reporter and the camera-man will never be very far distant from such a bed.

The mystics have all reported that their holy experiences are not capable of being put into words. Reflecting gloomily upon the falsehood, the *unreality* of most sexual 'realism', the publisher's reader comes to suspect that for good or for ill, the same is true of this other ecstasy; and he suggests to the aspiring novelist that distant delicate suggestion will very often be more effective, more truthful, than precise statement. Unless you are writing for a specifically pathological market, this will usually be good advice to follow.

In this connection, it needs to be pointed out that while sex can be comic or tragic or both, a preoccupation with lavatories is usually wearisome.

Humour of the excrementitious or stercoraceous kind can indeed exist and be workable. But apart from those of us who are very immature or slightly crazy, we tend to find its charm rather limited. Its appeal seems to vary inversely with the prevailing level of sanitation. The sanitary arrangements of Rabelais's time hardly bear thinking of; and to him, the subject was endlessly droll. Conversely, many present-day Americans of the wealthier sort fail to see how it could ever be funny at all. We Englishmen live at an intermediate point; that is to say, we usually have workable sanitation, but it tends to be a shade archaic and noisy and it doesn't always work. For us, therefore, there are definite possibilities of lavatory-humour.

But they are very limited: don't overwork them in the name of realism. Some bad novels are suffused all through, and quite pointlessly, with shafts of wit (as Dr Spooner might have said): it isn't much fun for the publisher's reader. An ounce of civet, good apothecary, to sweeten my imagination!

CHAPTER NINE

MEET MY FOLKS

IF YOU ALLOW it to become known that you are writing a novel, various friends will approach you at once, looking coy. "And are you going to put *me* into it?" they will ask.

The only prudent answer will be a flat No; any admission, any evasion will land you in trouble later on, and not only in connection with your less pleasant characters and the risk of a libel action. Few people like the idea of being exhibited to the world in a novel: it is something of an embarrassment and an affront to discover suddenly that one has been coldly scrutinised and objectively recorded, even in flattering terms. We don't like to think of ourselves as *objects*.

But to the novelist, everybody he meets is an object, and that hurried No will never be wholly sincere. Towards the people he meets, his attitude is always predatory. He will seldom capture them straightforwardly, for unmodified display in his next book; but he is always hungry, always ready to fling something new into the stockpot that simmers permanently inside his head.

If the characters in your novel are to carry conviction and hold our interest, they will need to be based upon your own experience of individuals and of human nature in general. But before you serve them up to your readers, you will have to submit them to a good deal of cookery and development and elaboration. Failure to do this is often responsible for the thin, the 'cardboard' characters who populate unworkable novels so boringly. Their creators have merely copied down what they knew of individuals, and it wasn't enough. We never know very much about other people; and even a good biographer, whose task is made easier by a mass of documentation about his subject, will not acquire the novelist's kind of knowledge. "People in real life hardly seem to be definite enough to appear in print," says Ivy Compton-Burnett. "People are too elusive, too shadowy to be copied," says Somerset Maugham, "and they are also too incoherent and contradictory." "They aren't simple enough," adds Joyce Cary: "Look at all the great heroes and heroines . . . they are essentially characters from fable, and so they must be to take their place in a formal construction which is to have meaning."

The characters in your novel will thus have a general difference from the people you have met: they will be more clear and simple, and they will need to be much more thoroughly known than real people are ever known by anybody. Upon this impossible kind of knowledge, the plausibility or 'realism' of your characters—and therefore of your entire novel —will chiefly depend: the unconvincing or 'cardboard' character is, in general, the one whom the novelist didn't know very well.

This imposes upon you a task of going very deeply into human nature, by a process that combines accurate observation with understanding and intelligent guesswork. "Novelists differ from the rest of the world," says Virginia Woolf, "because they do not cease to be interested in character when they have learnt enough about it for practical purposes." "Now we can get a definition as to whether a character in a book is real," says Forster: "It is real when the novelist knows everything about it. He may not choose to tell us all he knows . . ."

This last point is important. The good novelist operates from a position of strength: he has undeployed reserves: he could tell us a great deal more about each of his principal characters than will ever be directly and obviously relevant to his story. Unconsciously and unintentionally, he will no doubt cause some of this extra knowledge to be implied in the novel, and these faint implications will give depth and roundness. But apart from this, his own confidence, his overall plausibility will be guaranteed by the fact that he knows what he's talking about.

Other applications of the same principle are familiar to us. The good teacher is one who knows his subject thoroughly: he explains the rudiments well because he sees them against a background of full depth and complexity. An ignorant teacher will not be efficient. By frantic homework, he may contrive to keep just one lesson ahead of the class, and in a sense, they will then be told everything that they need to know. But it will be conveyed to them from a position of weakness, and therefore in a lame and dull fashion.

You will always find it hard to be interesting about subjects or individuals that are only thinly known to you. And therefore, as Somerset Maugham says, "you can never know enough about your characters". You must brood over them endlessly in depth, in ways often remote from the action of your novel. Let us suppose that your story concerns early adult life alone: if it were suddenly asked of you, could you be interesting and informative about the long-forgotten childhood of each principal character? about the pimply adolescence of your bland and confident young executive? about the particular old age that awaits your now-blossoming heroine? Could you say, with the confidence born of familiarity, how each would behave in some totally different situation, utterly unlike anything proposed for the novel?

You may find it helpful to prepare, for your own private use, a long rambling incoherent essay about each of your principal characters, including all sorts of personal details and memories and responses and characteristics, ranging far beyond the limits of the story. The actual writing of such an essay may not be necessary: you may be able to work it all out and hold it in your head. But before the end, your knowledge of each principal character must have become so wide and deep that if you chose to write that essay—a fairly complete biographical and psychological study of the individual in question—you could do it easily.

This knowledge will be complex and full of ambiguities. In the first instance, it will concern the actual 'truth' about the person in question, as seen from the point of view of your own God-like wisdom. But it will also concern the limited and unreliable ideas that your various characters have about themselves and about each other. From the interplay of these various half-truths and illusions, your novel will gain a great deal of its power.

Next time you see a couple of lovers, wholly wrapped up in each other upon a park bench, remember that there are no less than six characters present, and that they would all need to be taken into account if this apparently simple situation were to be wholly described. There's the man as he actually is; there's the girl as she actually is; there's his idea of her and her idea of him; there's his idea of himself and her idea of herself. Your novel contains more people than you suppose. If in the literal sense there are n characters within it, all more or less embroiled with each other, the total number of persons and quasi-persons involved will be $n(n + 1)$. And this kind of algebra involves no constants: everything will be shifting and developing all the time.

Your understanding of all these characters and their relationships may well come slowly, in the course of your writing: in this respect as otherwise, the novelist embarks upon an exploration, desiring to find out about some people who are distantly and perhaps erroneously apprehended to begin with. Many novelists have undergone, and have described for our benefit, an experience that illustrates this important principle, while also reminding us once again that preconceived plots and plans, if they are prepared at all, must not be taken too seriously. On the face of it, there's a certain absurdity in what they say. Characters, they tell us, tend to get out of control; they turn out to have wills of their own; and insist on going their own way, to the annoyance of their creator, who had very laboriously worked out precise plans for their conduct and their future.

This may sound like sheer whimsy: how can a fictitious

character have a will of his own and defy his creator, his manipulator? "When I first planned my novel, I wanted Sophonisba to marry Eustace: the whole structure depended on this. But she turned out to be an awkward girl, and she wasn't having it: she dithered around for some time, and in the end she insisted on marrying Leopold. It put me to any amount of trouble! Confound the girl." If you hear a novelist talking like this, you may suspect that he's trying to be funny. Perhaps he is. But he may also be describing in the only language available to him—he isn't a philosopher or a psychologist—a prime fact about the creative process as actually experienced and about the relationship between an author and his characters.

We can describe this phenomenon in terms slightly more scientific, if we choose to. That novelist had in his subconscious mind an idea of 'Sophonisba' that was only present to his conscious mind—his thinking and planning mind—in very limited and inaccurate fashion. About this idea, he was therefore able to make factual mistakes when he was at the planning stage. But in the process of writing, his unconscious idea of Sophonisba became increasingly conscious, increasingly precise and capable of being put into accurate words; and this process showed up the mistakes that he'd made earlier on. They weren't mistakes about an actual girl—Sophonisba doesn't exist, even though she may be 'based on fact'—but they will feel as though they were.

In this semi-whimsical sense, Sophonisba knows what she's doing better than the author does. If by brute force and ignorance he forces her to marry Eustace, despite her blubbering protests, he will be introducing a falsity: she will be acting out of character, and the story won't ring true.

The point can be illustrated by a theological analogy. In the world of his story, the novelist plays the part of God, creating and disposing all things: he is, in an obvious sense, all-powerful. Even so, his creatures have a destiny that can only be fulfilled in a kind of freedom: they have to be given their heads, allowed to find their own way, in spite of the trouble they cause. Every theology has to provide for both freewill and predestination, must see God as the victim of the human race as well as its manager; and these paradoxes are echoed in the mini-theology of the novel, the relationship between the harassed creative novelist and his loved but tiresome characters.

He creates them in his own image and likeness: it has often been said, and in a certain sense truly, that no novelist ever portrays any individual except himself. He may not know much about other people, but at least he has a certain self-knowledge, most inaccurate in all probability but very loving and attentive. His creative question is "What shall Sophonisba do now?"; but in practice it often resolves itself into "What would *I* do now, if I were Sophonisba?"

He must therefore be able to identify with every character, to see it sympathetically from the inside. This may be difficult if he has a partisan and disapproving kind of mentality: if he is so afflicted, he should probably cause the characters whom he disapproves of most strongly to play only minor parts in his novel.

Even the most awful people make sense to themselves: in his own eyes, even the most hideous criminal seems well-justified in his conduct. If only people would try to *understand*!

The novelist must try to understand: he must identify. This may be easier than it seems. If you feel total hatred and contempt for some individual or some type, this top-level and conspicuous attitude of yours will often conceal a substratum or undercurrent of admiration and envy. Uncover this, and give it play: otherwise you will never be able to present that individual or that type convincingly. You have within you the makings of a saint, a hero, and other people naturally see you in that light; but you also have within you the makings of a whore, a traitor, a concentration-camp butcher, and the writing of your novel may well involve some imaginative fulfilment of these potentialities. You are engaged in a somewhat dirty and

dangerous trade: you will be uncovering certain parts of yourself that might be best left covered, and schizophrenia is an
occupational risk.

Apart from himself, and more obviously, a novelist draws
upon his experiences of other people. He can do this fruitfully
in a narrow and constricted way: "In no book," says Forster,
"have I got down more than the people I like, the person I
think I am, and the people who irritate me." But usually he
will range more widely; and in certain cases, his purposes will
be served by the closest possible representation of a living
individual, or maybe of several. The *roman à clef* is a perfectly
valid thing, though specialised in a direction that's commonly
satirical, and a shade risky in terms of libel.

Most characters in fiction are generated by a process that's
slower, more complex, less direct. "I do not take, and have
never taken, either action or characters directly from life," says
Moravia; "Events may suggest events to be used in a work
later; similarly, persons may suggest future characters; but
suggest is the word to remember." Trollope says that if the
novelist is to paint a picture worthy of attention, "the canvas
should be crowded with real portraits, not of individuals known
to the author, but of created persons impregnated with traits
of character which are known." The novelist is certainly a
body-snatcher, but his friends and acquaintances need not be
too apprehensive: he will often make off with a leg or an eye,
but seldom with an entire carcase. "A useful trick," says Forster,
"is to look back upon [a real person] with half-closed eyes, fully
describing certain characteristics. I am left with about two-thirds
of a human being, and can get to work. A likeness isn't aimed at
and couldn't be attained, because a man's only himself amidst
the particular circumstances of his life and not amid other
circumstances. . . . When all goes well, the original material
soon disappears, and a character who belongs to the book and
nowhere else emerges." Very often a character is assembled
piecemeal, the novelist working upon grouped elements of
diverse origin. "Characters come to me . . . when people are

talking to me," says Angus Wilson. "I feel I have heard this tone of voice in other circumstances. And, at the risk of seeming rude, I have to hold on to this and chase it back until it clicks with someone I've met before. The second secretary at the embassy in Bangkok may remind me of the chemistry assistant at Oxford. And I ask myself, what have they in common? Out of such mixtures I can create characters: all my life I've always known a lot of people."

The novelist must indeed be well acquainted with humanity. But the decisive thing here is the quality rather than the quantity of his experience: he does not need to be on familiar terms with diplomats at Bangkok and academics at Oxford. Novels get rejected for many reasons, but very seldom on account of the author's limited experience of humanity and the world. An observant openness to the people you meet is indeed necessary, but a wide-ranging and colourful kind of life is not. It can help, of course.

One frequently meets people who aspire to write novels, but hold back because of a feeling that they've lived too mousey and circumscribed an existence, never having splashed around and hit the great world in all its colour and variety. "What, *me* write a novel? But I've never been anywhere, I've never done anything!" Taken literally, such a disclaimer must always be untrue: the speaker cannot avoid having lived in certain places, met certain people, and undergone certain experiences. Given some degree of maturity, every one of us has accumulated enough adult experience to fill several novels.

In such a case, what sounds like a rather engaging kind of humility is in fact a gross illusion about what novels are. You will become a competent novelist by virtue of the quality of your response to experience, and to people in particular, rather than by virtue of any glamorous splendour and variety that your experience may have. Dull life in a pedestrian environment, seen through the right eyes and set forth by the right hand, can—and often does—take on the quality that publishers and their readers are looking for. "Provincialism does not signify in a writer, and may indeed be his chief source of strength," says Forster; "only a prig or a fool would complain that Defoe is cockneyfied or Thomas Hardy countryfied."

Don't blame your environment or the kind of life you lead : if you fail to write an excellent novel, the reason won't lie there. Is life in your dim suburb really so very much more circumscribed and petty than Jane Austen's life was at Chawton? Or is it just that you are less witty than she was, less sharply observant? Your neighbours may be less dull than you suppose. Such an expression as "normal, ordinary, dull people" means little more than "people I don't know much about".

In recent years, provincial or regional sub-cultures have gained a new confidence, at the expense of whatever is metropolitan, and for reasons partly literary : if you were brought up in Slagtown and are familiar with no other environment, you are now less likely to feel inferior on that account. You may even feel conceited about it. Even so, you may still need to be reminded that your own experience does already contain the raw material that you need for a novel. Many writers overstrain themselves, seeking to exploit a breadth and glamour of experience not their own, ignoring resources that already lie close to hand. It's uneconomic of them; and it often leads to falsity and failure.

This principle can be over-stated. Experience of a varied and colourful kind, such as those lucky people enjoy who go everywhere and do everything, *may* help you : it will certainly widen your repertoire, opening the door to various novel-sorts that would otherwise lie beyond your reach, and an exotic or surprising background may help to secure a pass-mark for a novel that would otherwise just fail to make the grade. But it won't always work out like that. Travel doesn't always broaden the mind, nor does a busy and varied social life : too many people and places and happenings may deaden your imaginative response instead of heightening it. The people who get around aren't always the interesting ones, in person or on paper : sometimes they only do this getting around because they're bored and fretful, and can't bear to sit still in one place. So they go round the world and see everything, they're flung out of brothels in New Orleans and they dine with cannibals in New Guinea, and they're still bored.

The quality and liveliness of your own response to experience —of whatever kind—is going to be the decisive thing. Don't let the writing of your novel be put off until you've won the pools and seen the world.

It may quite possibly need to be postponed, however, until you've grown a little older. Things aren't altogether easy for the very young novelist. His experience is commonly limited in a way that really is damaging : there isn't enough of it, and it hasn't been simmered sufficiently in the stockpot of memory and imagination. He tends to over-dramatise the things that occupy his present horizons, in a fashion sometimes endearing and sometimes absurd; and since he often has a confident hunger for large visions and ideas, he tends to produce the over-stretched novel—insufficient material, used too ambitiously. All this gets sorted out as he grows older, and in the meantime, it's very forgiveable. A publisher takes the long view, and is anxious to spot and secure a useful career in its fumbling earlier stages : his reader's toleration is extended accordingly.

Your novel, if it's to be a good one, will have to be written out of a well-stocked mind. In so far as it stands in close relation to fact, it must of course be based also upon precise and recent observation; and this can be very valuable. Enthusiasm for the novel, considered as pure imaginative creation, should not blind you to the possibilities, the value of a soundly informative or documentary element in fiction. Your story may therefore involve you in much homework of the factual kind; you may have to undertake research in libraries and on the spot, you may have to interrogate people, you may have to take photographs and buy local histories and accumulate all kinds of factual information. But in so far as your novel appeals to the imagination rather than to the factual curiosity, a different approach is necessary: here, in what will usually be the most important part of your task, you must depend upon that mental stockpot of yours, and for events and places no less than for people.

The important thing, as with an actual *pot-au-feu*, is that it should be simmered slowly and for a long time. "Remote memories, already distorted by the imagination," says Elizabeth Bowen, "are most useful for the purposes of scene. Unfamiliar or once-seen places yield more than do familiar often-seen places." The same is true of characters and events; and many novels fail because they are based upon experience too recent, raw, insufficiently digested, superficial. Give your experience time to sink in and ripen before you use it: don't write entirely, or chiefly, from the surface of your conscious mind. Thin stuff is bred in that way.

You should be wary, therefore, about any urge that you may feel towards the keeping of a notebook. This may seem a very sensible thing to do: surely the novelist has to gather his materials? Surely many of his best ideas will be lost if he doesn't keep a notebook?

There is plainly something in this. But you shouldn't worry too much about the loss of individual ideas: if you are in the right and fertile state of mind, there are plenty more where those ones came from. That notebook is a somewhat dangerous thing, and for two reasons. In the first place, you may find yourself drafting odd scraps of description and narrative and dialogue which then seem so splendid that you don't want to waste them; then, writing your novel at a later stage, you may strain and rupture its delicate fabric in your anxiety to insert these pre-existing plums of good writing. The diagnostic eye of the publisher's reader is familiar with the traumatic lesions that too often result from this kind of imprudence. In the second place, you may come to look upon your notebook as a substitute for that mental stockpot of memory and imagination; you may come to suppose that you're doing something immensely useful and constructive when you take voluminous notes. This will only seldom and marginally be the case. Your novel can't be written from anything except a well-stocked mind : and there isn't any labour-saving substitute for the actual burdensome writing of it.

Your notebook can be a splendid aid to self-deception : it can help you to think of yourself as 'a writer' when in fact you're producing nothing whatever, nor moving in any perceptible degree towards production. A writer is a man who writes : not a man who makes wonderful preparations for writing.

The weight of qualified opinion seems to be against the note-book. "I tried to keep one," says Dorothy Parker, "but I never could remember where I put the damn thing. I always say I'm going to keep one tomorrow." "At one time," says Truman Capote, "I used to keep notebooks with outlines for stories. But I found doing this somehow deadened the idea in my imagina-tion. If the notion is good enough, if it truly belongs to *you*, then you can't forget it—it will haunt you till it's written." Forster insists, stiffly, that he does *not* keep a notebook : "I should feel it improper." Thornton Wilder once confessed to the keeping of a journal : "but I never re-read those entries".

Used cautiously, a notebook can serve two purposes. It can record factual data that you are going to need later; and by the mere act of writing, it can catch fugitive thoughts and engrave them into the mind, though not necessarily into the conscious memory. You might do best to keep two notebooks : one of the factual kind, to be referred to as necessary, and one of that imaginative and thought-catching variety, never to be referred to at all. Tear its pages out and burn them as they become filled : don't let such notes get an exaggerated idea of their own dignity and permanence.

Your characters, therefore, and the other ingredients that go to make up your novel, must emerge and be presented in well-simmered form. The raw novel, the underdone novel, is an offence to the reader's palate and a strain upon his digestion : typescripts are often rejected for no reason more precise than this. In such a case, the author's best policy will be to brood over it for another year and then to write it again.

This slow cookery naturally and necessarily effects a transformation. The end-product is very different from raw experience : even when it's of the kind that we call 'realistic', a novel is not—in any simple sense—'like life'. And this is especially true of the characters in it. The inhabitants of the novel-world are, in most cases, recognisably human; but they are not like the ordinary run of real people. Considered as members of the human race, they are a specialised and highly untypical minority, qualified to hold office in the novel-world because of the interesting things that can plausibly be represented as happening to them, the unusual element of unpredictability in their lives. They started off, perhaps, as your own dull neighbours; but then they had to be changed, disciplined, groomed, and adapted.

This means, in the first place, that the statistical distribution of age-groups within the novel-world is unlike what we find elsewhere. People in stories tend to be young adults, over eighteen and under forty : in the novel-world, this age-group is over-represented, and for an obvious reason. Before they reach the age of eighteen or so, real people tend to be tied down to the routines of home and school or very junior employment : after forty, they tend to be set in their ways. But between these two ages, the element of uncertainty or potentiality in their lives is at its highest, in matters of love and marriage very conspicuously, but in countless other matters as well. This uncertainty or potentiality is what the novelist needs : in the development and then the resolution of it, his whole art is contained. Older or younger people offer him less scope. "The world's anguish," says Faulkner, "is caused by people between twenty and forty," and anguish, of course, is bread-and-butter to the novelist.

In various other ways, the population of the novel-world is sharply different from the people we actually meet. More of the girls are beautiful, for one thing, and far more of them are available. Relatively few people are enslaved to routine and conformity : those who are so enslaved are usually there to provide a contrast or else to astonish us by breaking out. People abound who lead unpredictable lives : this landscape is crowded with the rich, the unstable, the independently creative, the eccentric, the footloose. And their experience is concentrated. They are very much involved with lovers and close friends : their attention is not diffused, as yours and mine is, over a wide penumbra of casual acquaintances. Moments of stress and decision come frequently, acutely, in clear-cut fashion : frontier-situations proliferate, with abstract issues becoming concrete and urgent. On all sides there is a swiftness of action, an intensity of response : things happen and are deeply felt, developments move on swiftly towards climax. Not much work gets done, and very little routine work : money and the absence of it are seldom daily preoccupations. Within this world, very little can be seen of the vague messy torpor in which most people actually live for most of the time.

This is a mercy. If any novel actually contrived a precise photographic resemblance to real life, it would make wretched reading : it would be intolerably dull and diffuse.

This principle applies with particular force to dialogue, upon which the presentation of your characters and the movement and pace of your novel will very largely depend.

In one sense, dialogue must obviously be realistic. Your characters, if we are to believe in them, must speak with the voices of living people; and you will be a poor novelist unless you can develop an accurate and retentive ear for the patterns, the rhythms, the endless varieties of everyday speech. Where this qualification is absent, the reader's report will speak severely of stilted and unnatural dialogue, and often of a consequent general deadness in the characters and therefore in the story.

But here again, the concept of 'realism' can be taken too literally. In the dialogue more than in any other respect, the novel cannot be simply a photographic record of experience. Bookish talk won't do in everyday life, and real talk won't do for books.

It would be easy—though ill-mannered—to verify this by experiment. Let a tape-recorder be hidden in some room where people are likely to be engaged in important conversation; and afterwards, let the result be typed out word for word, with all the usual novel-rubrics of quotation-marks and *he said* and *she replied* and the rest of it. A document so obtained would be a strictly realistic record of actual conversation; and except in very rare cases, it would be completely useless as a novel-sequence. It would be impossibly diffuse, and it would convey to us only the verbal element of a complex happening that was non-verbal in many respects: taken out of their context, the mere words would become dry and empty and insufficient. That tape-recorder would catch only the bones of the conversation, or perhaps its ghost.

The dramatist, of stage or screen, can be much more 'realistic' with dialogue than the novelist can. He knows that the actor, having studied the part in advance, will be able to supplement the bare words with the non-verbal elements that contribute to any real conversation—that is to say, with intonation, expression, and gesture. And in a play or story written for sound radio, intonation (though not expression or gesture) can be supplied in the same way.

The novelist, however, has to rely on the bare words alone: there is no interpreter to give life and body to them. Within limits, he can of course supply a running commentary upon the dialogue: he can place on record his characters' inflexions and tones of voice, their facial expressions, their gestures. But he usually needs to be very abstemious in this respect: otherwise, his dialogue will get bogged down in adverbs and adverbial clauses, and this will often be tedious.

He therefore needs to have at his disposal the art of writing dialogue that seems quite natural and realistic while being in fact highly stylised. The mere words will have much more work to do than in actual conversation: they will have to be un-naturally precise and revealing. With little help from outside, they must carry a heavy load of meaning, and without vagueness or ambiguity, even when the speech of confused and ignorant people is being represented. And good dialogue is well marshalled: it may very often suggest, but it should never possess, the chaotic repetitive slovenly incoherence of our real-life jabberings.

The novelist starts with natural speech-patterns, and he certainly needs to be a close observer of these: they will be incessantly suggested and echoed in his writing. But he cannot dish them up raw: novel-talk serves purposes quite distinct from the purposes of real talk. In particular, it advances the action.

Nothing is easier to write than a long slab of waffle-dialogue that gets us nowhere. Most real-life conversation does get us nowhere, and this doesn't matter at all. But the aspiring novelist must take care not to include within his pages anything that approaches the condition of padding: his dialogue, in particular, must be an onward movement. After each exchange of words, things must be slightly different. "During dialogue," says Elizabeth Bowen, "the characters confront one another . . . What is being said is the effect of something that has happened; at the same time, what is being said *is in itself something happening,* which will, in turn, leave its effect . . . Short of a small range of physical acts—a fight, murder, love-making—dialogue is the most vigorous and visible inter-action of which characters in a novel are capable. Speech is what the characters *do to each other."*

This is the prime requirement. Your novel cannot afford to carry passenger-items that don't pay their way: your dialogue must justify itself, revealing character, advancing the action. Mere realism is not enough.

But it is still necessary. The novelist needs to keep his feet on the ground, his eyes and ears receptively open at all times. In his attitude towards the spoken language, let him be the one party-guest who stays observantly sober when all the others are flown with insolence and wine: in his attitude towards humanity at large, let him resemble the man who went to a strip-tease performance in order to watch the audience.

161

CHAPTER TEN

A MACHINE FOR PLEASING

So far, you have managed not to alienate the publisher's reader. In a well-mannered and appropriate fashion, you have been conducting him through a landscape of some novelty and interest, populated by characters in whom he has found it possible to believe, in whose affairs he has become suitably involved. Let us say that the content of your novel is satisfactory.

But any work of art involves form as well as content: like a poem, a novel not only *means* but *is*. It needs to give pleasure as a thing made, not merely as a thing said. Whatever else he may do, the able novelist has to conduct his readers through an ordered pattern or structure of experience that will have its own rightness and will offer to them its own abstract but deep kind of satisfaction.

This is of course a somewhat artificial distinction: a novel exists as a whole, it functions or fails to function as a whole. Content and form are different sides of the same coin: if one were altered, the other would change as well. In any good artefact, meaning and design are inextricably entangled, each defining the other. A good writer does not first set forth a solid straightforward plum-cake of meaning, and then decorate it with the separate and ornamental sugar-icing of 'good style'; and in the same way, the novelist should not think of the form and the content of his novel as though these were two separate things. They are two ways of talking about the same thing.

Both are important; and in revising your novel before you submit it for publication, you should attend to both aspects of the matter. Your main concern may possibly be for your novel's subject-matter and its authenticity; in these days, when subjectivism is in fashion and when art is so widely equated with self-expression, your natural instinct will probably tend in this direction. If only to redress the balance, you should therefore remember that you are making as well as saying : your work must stand up to criticism in terms of craftsmanship. "I need to work with my hands," says Simenon, "I would like to carve my novel in a piece of wood." Try to develop this instinct, this sentiment, if you don't possess it already. Attend to the structure and shape of what you're making, quite as much as to the authenticity and power of what you're saying. Countless novels say things that are true and deep and interesting, but are rejected on grounds of shapelessness, of structural weakness.

If the technological fallacy were not a fallacy, it would now be possible to set forth a series of well-tried structural principles, by the strict observance of which a sound novel might easily and certainly be constructed. Unfortunately, this cannot be done : the art is too varied and multiple, raising unique problems in every case. The novelist has to feel his way : in the last resort, this matter can only be judged intuitively. The main thing is that it *should* be judged, and seriously, at one stage or another. When a novel fails by reason of bad craftsmanship, bad structure, bad stage-management, the publisher's reader often feels that the author has approached these questions thoughtfully but dealt with them clumsily. Just as often, however, he feels that the author has simply not attended seriously enough to this aspect of his task. It isn't precisely that he has failed as a craftsman and designer : it's rather that he hasn't tried.

At various stages in the revision of your novel, you should therefore stand back and look critically upon the artefact that is coming to shape in your hands. Quite apart from the subject-matter, is it a well-made *thing*? Does it look right? Is it well-balanced? Are its proportions pleasing to the eye? Are the parts suitably related to the whole? Does it hang together, constituting a unity in all its variety?

The important thing is that such questions should be active in your mind. It doesn't matter if you lack any basis for a

theoretical and systematic answering of them. When your novel
has become famous, a theoretically-minded critic will be able to
analyse and explain its structure, its design, its mechanical functioning. But at the time of writing, all this will be a mystery to
you, a matter of groping and fumbling and instinctive or intuitional judgment. If you really are a potential novelist, this will
see you through, and fruitfully, where set rules and formulas—
if they could be found—might cripple or sterilise you. But this
instinctive or intuitional judgment needs to be given a chance :
it must be brought to bear upon the formal or structural aspects
of your novel—by effort and self-discipline if necessary—quite
as much as upon its content.

None the less, if no positive rules for the workmanlike design
and construction of novels are available, the publisher's reader
may still be able to help : he can offer certain comments, based
upon his experiences of failure in this respect.

He would remind you, in the first instance, that a story-teller
pleases his readers by establishing, developing, and finally resolving a certain tension or suspense in their minds. In his opening
pages, the novelist is concerned to establish this tension or
suspense, to get us interested; in the main body of his book, he
faces complex problems of sustaining and developing and vary-
ing it, with various partial resolutions and various new complica-
tions; finally, he has to achieve something like a climax and a
resolution. Thus he will achieve his three main purposes. He
wanted us to be attracted by his novel and drawn into it : he
didn't want us to drop it half-way through; and at the end, he
wanted us to have an agreeable sensation of achieved finality,
and to look back with pleasure upon the experience of reading
what he wrote.

His structural problem is concerned with the manipulation of
this stress or tension in our minds; and this needs some attention.
It can take many different forms : for brevity and convenience,
let us call it 'the question'. That term will remind us that a novel

is essentially an interrogative thing—an asking, a quest, an exploration.

At the heart of your novel, there may indeed lie a simple question of fact: who did the murder? will our hero win through? But often, or usually, something much more complex and undefinable than that will be involved: your 'question' will be an uncertainty, an involvement, an anxiety in our minds, a split or contradiction within our hopes and sympathies, a tease of our emotions. It will provide us with a temporary and vicarious unhappiness, ludicrously small or frighteningly large in its scope, dexterously developed and sustained within us and resolved at the end: for whatever psychological reasons, this pattern of experience is found to be pleasurable.

In a short story, the pattern will be a simple one: normally, a single 'question' will arise, be intensified, and finally reach something that can be called an answer: direct or oblique, ambiguous or ironic in many cases, but still an answer. But the novelist works in more complex fashion. He raises a number of 'questions', causing them to overlap and interweave in various ways; and he will usually provide or imply a single over-riding 'question', related to all of the others, resolved or answered towards the end.

The word 'question' needs to be kept in quotation-marks, to remind us that something more than a simple question of fact will usually be involved. Neither the author nor his readers will necessarily be able to explain it precisely in words: on both sides, it may be experienced only as a vague undefinable stress or unease in the imagination or the emotions.

But this element of 'question' must always be present, and in a fashion that's active, complex, and dynamic. Every scene, every page in your novel must develop the pattern, playing with these 'questions' or uncertainties, resolving some and establishing others, conducting us forward—by a route that will possibly be very circuitous—towards the ultimate resolution or reply that will conclude the novel.

It is in this sense that a novelist needs to keep the ball rolling.

At every stage our interest must be held, we must be given a definite incentive to continue our reading : there must be no point at which we can lay the book aside without an uncomfortable feeling of unresolved suspense. The ship must be kept under way, the onward pressure of the story must be maintained. As long as some kind of question or tension or suspense is actively on the move, your story will live; where nothing of the kind is happening, it will die for the time being.

This kind of movement is the key thing : continued emotional and imaginative involvement is what matters. 'Action', in the more obvious sense, is very important indeed; but it is only important as a means to that end. Your novel can easily grind to a standstill, it can become stagnant and die, even at a point where your pages are crowded with tumultuous outward happenings : conversely, there can be a steady and splendid onward pressure in the total absence of such tumult. The 'unputdownable' novel is quite often the novel in which nothing very much seems to happen.

Two mistakes are commonly made here by inexperienced writers. One writer will rely too heavily upon simple action, ignoring the greater need for movement and 'question' : the publisher's reader will then complain that he has been overwhelmed with data, while not being given any reason for taking an interest in it. The story is there, and often deafeningly, but it evokes a weak response or none at all. Another novelist—more sophisticated, more abstemious—will offer the *stagnant* novel : one 'question' will be mounted before our eyes, and then we'll be invited simply to gaze upon it for an extended period. A still photograph cannot serve the purpose of a film.

A novel is an onward movement through time : it exists in the time-dimension as music does, not in the space-dimensions as painting and sculpture do. From this fact, a very important principle follows. The novelist must always concern himself with processes rather than with states : by instinct or by effort, he must be in sympathy with the evolutionary or developmental habit of mind that has characterised the period of the novel's greatness. He must look before and after, eyeing the continuum of antecedents and consequences: 'the present moment', severed from past and future and captured as in a snapshot, must always strike him as a somewhat unreal abstraction. Very often indeed, his failure can be diagnosed in terms of an excessive interest in state, an inadequate attention to process. Sometimes he will devise an excellent situation and then just talk about it, so that the novel never gets moving; sometimes he will devise a series of separate static *tableaux*, linking them mechanically, so that the novel becomes a succession of snapshots where it should have had the movement, the continuity of a film.

Keep the ball rolling: think in terms of time and process. Every scene, every happening in your novel is the consequence of countless things that have happened previously in your characters' lives and the cause of countless things that will happen afterwards, though only a few of these will be shown to the reader. Your characters are human, living in time, rocketing forward at the terrifying speed of 3,600 seconds per hour, with birth receding into the distance and death approaching. If twelve months pass in the course of your narrative, each of these people will be one year older afterwards, and will have suffered a year's experience and a year's changes.

A good novel is a working-out of possibilities, a continuously-sustained vicarious engagement with the experience of time, the resolution of freedom into destiny; and this is equally true of a schoolboy's adventure story and the most rarefied exploration of psychological subtlety. Let the novelist make sure that this engagement is sustained, that some process and 'question' is constantly on the move: let him remember that the word 'static' tends to recur in readers' reports, and that it tends to damn.

If a hostile critic were to open your book at random, and rudely ask you "What new thing is here supposed to be teasing and bothering the reader, and thus making it impossible for him to lay the book aside at this particular point?" an answer must always be available. You may not be able to put it into words, but it must be there. Before your novel is finalised, submit

it to a process of random checking on these lines. Remember
that to the publisher's reader, it constitutes *work* : let him not
look back upon it as drudgery.

The simplicity of this single and changeless requirement should
not distract you, however, from something very different—the
need for variety and contrast. In your novel, as in any work of
art, unity must co-exist in complex counterpoint with multiplicity.

People have limited staying-power, and the mind appreciates
a fairly frequent change of task and surroundings. Look after
this requirement of ours: be compassionate towards our weakness. Your novel must engage us constantly with movement and
'question', but the intensity and the mode of this engagement
must vary. We cannot be kept at fever-pitch the whole time.
The publisher's reader often comes across a novel that begins at
a deafening emotional and verbal *fortissimo,* and maintains that
volume relentlessly until the end. After a few pages he's punch-
drunk, hardly able to notice what is happening. Another novel
will begin in a delicate muted way, *mezzo-piano,* speaking to us
in a water-colour sort of voice, very gently, and this will usually
be more promising. At least it offers the possibility of a sudden
new intensity. The novelist who has shouted from the very beginning is at a loss when his story calls for a new and climactic
loudness: his vocal cords are sore already, he has dissipated his
resources. If your normal conversation is a tissue of swear-words
and obscenity, you've got nothing to blaspheme *with* when things
get really terrible. And so this other and quieter novelist acts
more prudently: by raising his voice to a mere *mezzo-forte,* he
can create by contrast a shattering effect of loudness and still
have something in reserve. But very often he misses his chances:
he drones on in that original *mezzo-piano* for ever, soothing us
into a profound slumber where change and contrast would have
kept us awake.

There must be emotional differentiation within your novel.
There will be big scenes, moments of crisis, turning-points. At

such moments as these, there will have to be an intensity, a degree of emotional and imaginative engagement that cannot be sustained for very long. And in between these big moments, while movement and 'question' must continue, they may continue more gently, giving us something of a rest though still leading us forward. Let your tone of voice vary accordingly : don't let your novel be like a continuous high-pitched buzz, starting on the first page and switched off abruptly on the last, devoid of all contrast or relief; and don't let it be an endless flat mumble.

Our exploration takes us over mountainous country : there will be high spots, exciting and exhausting too, and between them there will be valleys where the going is easier. But each high spot points forward to the next. Intermediate resolutions must only be partial : do not fall into the mistake of the inexperienced novelist who ends his story in the middle, quite unintentionally, and then has to embark upon a cumbrous process of getting it into motion again, while the audience drift away.

There is a kind of development in daily life which at first seems likely to solve all our problems, but then turns out to have created more problems than it solved. A pattern more or less of this kind will be appropriate for your big scenes, your moments of crisis.

Seek variation in many modes. Your novel will consist of scene and summary : at one point your characters will be actually on-stage, doing things and saying things before our eyes, and at another point you will lay them aside for description, for summarised and recapitulatory statement, for background, for comment. Generally speaking, you will rely chiefly upon scene, for your major effects and your big moments at least. Summary is useful for the controlling of tempo and for the representation of any gradual process, but you can do without very much of it : many excellent novels consist almost wholly of scene. Usually, however, you will want to alternate scene with summary, if only for the sake of change and relief : remembering always that the transition from scene to summary (or *vice versa*) is a moment of particular danger. At that point, the reader's attention is likely

to wander—especially if you start your new scene with the vague
and deflating words "One day . . ." Be more precise than that
if you want to be believed: insist that it was the second Tuesday
in August.

But in your pursuit of variation and flexibility, your avoidance
of monotony, it will be unwise for you to place too much reliance
upon a frequent change of 'angle'. This device has been over-
worked: the publisher's reader gives a faint and ignoble groan
when he finds, once again, that this novel is told in the first
person throughout but by a variety of different characters. The
first chapter is headed 'Jim', and indeed it is Jim who speaks:
the second chapter is headed 'Mrs Slugthorpe', and we aren't
let down, we do get that lady's subtly different approach to the
same situation, and if it's a boring one it won't be any the less
boring because we've now seen it from two angles.

In general, the inexperienced novelist will do wisely if he
sticks to the straightforward third-person angle. The autobiographical or first-person angle is dangerous. It is too easy to do
badly, it opens the flood-gates of mere self-revelation: as Henry
James said, it "puts a premium on the loose, the improvised, the
cheap and easy."

But whatever angle you use, let it be used consistently. Lay
your relevant cards upon the table: don't withhold front-stage
information. If Mrs Slugthorpe is your angle-character for the
moment or permanently, if all things are being seen through her
eyes, from her point of view, in terms of her experience, then
be consistent and don't cheat. If things are said to her, we must
be allowed to hear them. Our sharing in her consciousness must
not be switched off for a moment, just so that you can create
an artificial mystery. Clumsy novelists often do this, and it's
infuriating. When you want to create a mystery, do it in some
way that doesn't cheat the reader of information that he was
entitled to expect.

A certain self-control may also be needed in connection with
the various tricks that can be played with the time-sequence. The
most obvious of these is the straight flash-back. According to

Ford Madox Ford, this time-shift—as he calls it—"delights everybody". Perhaps people were more easily delighted in those innocent days; certainly they had been less torrentially inundated with gratuitous and over-elaborate versions of that time-shift. At all events, you must not hope to delight people quite as simply and mechanically as that.

In this respect, and in connection with your stage-management in general, the thing to remember is that we've all become very sales-resistant by now. Tricks and gimmicks arouse our suspicions: if some product is urged upon us by the use of a very sophisticated sales technique, our first response will be a nasty suspicious feeling that the product itself can't be very good. And the publisher's reader has a weary and negative sort of mind : time and time again, he's met the author who supposes that mechanical trickeries—of one sort or another—will make up for imaginative and narrative weakness. Be careful not to arouse his prejudices.

The novelist can sometimes have excellent reasons for not telling his story in the natural order, with Friday following hot on the heels of Thursday and adolescence hot on the heels of childhood. "The flashback in my novels is not just a trick," says Joyce Cary. "In, for example, *The Moonlight,* I used it in order to make my theme possible. It was essential to compare two generations. You can't do that without a flashback contrast : the chronological run-through by itself is no good."

But, in general, be content to tell a simple story : begin at the beginning, go on to the end, then stop. If—like Joyce Cary— you find that your particular purpose can't be served quite as simply as that, then make what re-arrangements are necessary. But don't ever let the publisher's reader suspect that you've contorted and complicated up a simple narrative in order to conceal its nakedness or in order to appear clever.

Whatever technical devices you find it appropriate to use, everything will depend ultimately upon your basic ability in narrative and stage-management. In this connection, you should remember that while people don't believe everything they hear, they have a strong tendency to believe whatever they've seen, or whatever they suppose themselves to have seen. All conjuring depends upon this fact, and upon the further fact that people are very easily fooled into thinking they've seen something when in fact they haven't.

The old rule, therefore, still holds good: show, don't tell. There's no reason for us to believe what you say: you have come before us as a writer of fictions, a liar. But let the thing seem to happen before our eyes, and you'll have us hooked and credulous.

This principle is asserted in almost every book on the art of fiction, and it should hardly need further re-assertion now. "The novelist who doesn't represent, and represent all the time, is lost," said Henry James. "It strikes me," said Dickens in a letter to a fellow-novelist, "that you constantly hurry your narrative (and yet without getting on) by telling it, in a sort of impetuous breathless way, in your own person, when the people should tell it and act it for themselves. My notion always is, that when I have made the people to play out the play, it is, as it were, their business to do it, and not mine."

Old advice, and it should be familiar to the aspiring novelist. But even now, countless novels are weak and mushy in their impact, and are therefore rejected, because their authors were too ready to explain and assert and tell what we should have seen displayed in action.

Beware of flat statement: beware of sustained descriptive and explanatory passages: in particular, resist the temptation to give us long accounts of what people were thinking. If their thoughts deserve attention, let them become incarnate in words and deeds: for nine writers out of ten, this will be more prudent than any direct representation of those thoughts by means of a stream-of-consciousness technique. The fans have come to see some action: let them have it, and use it to manipulate their attention and interest, to guide them along the forest-paths that you have chosen. At every point, *cause* them to have the emotional response that is appropriate: don't just name it and instruct them to manufacture it for themselves. "Instead of telling us that a thing was 'terrible'," says C. S. Lewis, "describe it so that we'll be terrified. Don't say it was 'delightful', make *us* say 'delightful' when we've read the description. You see, all those words (horrifying, wonderful, hideous, exquisite) are only saying to your readers 'please will you do my job for me'."

Show, don't tell: work upon your readers, and chiefly by action, 'question', movement. If you can begin to see your task dramatically, in terms of stage or screen, this will very commonly be all to the good.

Sooner or later, you will have to bring your novel to a close. Let us hope that it makes a good end, and can then face the Judgment in confidence, avoiding the Hell of rejection, achieving the Heaven of publication.

In the ending of any good novel, there will be an element of inevitability and an element of surprise. We knew, in general terms, that we were making for the source of the Nile; but we didn't know where it would be found or what it would look like. When he finally closes your book, the reader must therefore respond to its ending in two ways. On the one hand, he must recognise this as the only possible ending to the story. It must have a rightness, it must seem beyond question to belong: in a real sense, it must turn out to have been implied from the start, with all happenings and all questionings working inevitably towards this particular resolution.

But this inevitability in your ending must only be apparent after the event. To the last, your story must remain unknown, unpredictable, a cluster of questionings that will close in and intensify towards the end, so that the reader is still engaged, and more deeply. Only seldom will it be prudent for you to offer a surprise-ending in the fullest sense, a shock-resolution on the very last page: nevertheless, as your reader approaches the end, he must feel a heightened sense of uncertainty, and in due course a definite feeling of surprise—of *pleased* surprise, even if the substance of your ending is tragic and agonising.

This is of course a highly artificial proceeding: it corresponds to nothing in our real-life experience, and it is not an easy thing to achieve. Forster stresses the difficulty and the artificiality too: "This, as far as one can generalise, is the inherent defect of novels: they go off at the end."

But however difficult and artificial it is, the task has to be attempted: you must cause your novel to end in some way that is both inevitable and unpredictable. Otherwise the publisher's reader will have some unkind things to say; and you must remember that the ending of your book is—naturally enough— the last part of it that he will read. It will stick in the top layer of his mind; it will be in the forefront of his memory when he sits down to write his report. You must not give a finally bad impression, in his eyes or—later on—in the eyes of the book-reviewers.

Don't let him say, therefore, that the conclusion of your book can be seen approaching from ten miles off: don't allow it to make its presence and nature known, blatantly, at too early a stage; don't let it appear upon the horizon, puffing and trumpeting and drawing attention to itself, while we're still only half-way through the story.

But on the other hand, don't let him say that your ending doesn't belong; that it was tacked on in an arbitrary and artificial fashion; that it isn't related—by a process of organic development, of worked-out implication and fulfilled potentiality —to the whole of what's gone before. Above all, don't let it depend upon the introduction of wholly new data: let there be no 'god from the machine', no good fairy appearing at the last minute to sort everything out by magic.

Very often indeed, and in a mood of exasperation, the publisher's reader finds himself making one of these serious objections to a novel that's otherwise first-class. They tend to damn; and matters cannot always be rectified by minor tail-end surgery.

These problems will always look after themselves if, like a good Christian, your novel conducts its whole life with its death-bed in view. Have that destination in mind, vaguely when you embark upon your first draft, more precisely as you undertake successive revisions; and in your final version, let the whole exploration be ordered towards an objective known to yourself and teasingly revealed to your readers as the surprising but inevitable goal of the entire journey. Thus pressure and movement will be maintained, and anti-climax avoided.

Many novels fail by not being properly ordered towards their ending. One will peter out in feebleness and irresolution; another will drag itself along more and more wearily as it gets older, as if the author wanted to put it out of its misery but couldn't think how; another will prattle along emptily and happily, as if the author had quite run out of ideas but couldn't bear to stop talking.

There will be interludes and diversions in your novel, pauses for rest and refreshment, campfires, agreeable parleyings with the natives. But let your eyes and your heart be set always upon that distant source of the Nile, that land of heart's desire, that consummation, that death.

Your novel, an utterance of your private and unique self, is also a machine for pleasing other people: let it be constructed with this fact in mind. There is multiplicity, of course, in the concept of 'pleasing'. The sound of that word may suggest a slight and milky kind of gratification, whereas your novel may well 'please' its readers by shattering their nerves, or baffling them with riddles, or harrowing them with the world's grief and despair. People can be pleased in a great many different ways, some of them savouring of masochism and the death-wish.

But however the word is to be understood in your particular case, your central task is of this nature. "The writer of stories must please, or he will be nothing," says Trollope. There is a certain paradox here. Of some thoroughly objectionable character, it is often said that he "doesn't make the slightest attempt to please other people". This is a serious charge: on the other hand, conscious and systematic attempts to please, to ingratiate oneself, to give a good impression, will often be worse than useless.

In most cases, the chief danger for the aspiring novelist will be that extraneous purposes may distract him from his primary task of giving pleasure by narrative. These extraneous purposes may be very sound and laudable in their way : none the less, they will endanger a novel's success if not kept in their place.

The novelist may, for example, have been charged with a burning desire to tell us the truth about the universe, or to convert us to the true religion. He may have wanted to call attention to some public or social wrong, and thus to mobilise public opinion. He may have wanted to express himself, to communicate, to ease the burden of his personal loneliness; he may have wanted to let off steam, to externalise the turmoil in his head, to "Cleanse the stuff'd bosom of that perilous stuff Which weighs upon the heart." He may have wanted to earn for himself a place in literary history by starting an astonishing new trend, a new chapter in the evolution of The Novel. He may have wanted a pretext for gloating over sex and violence. He may have wanted to express some kind of partisanship, praising one faction and denouncing another. He may have wanted to serve and interpret and propitiate 'the spirit of the age'. He may have wanted to tell us about some unusual mode of existence, experienced or dreamt up by himself. He may have wanted to talk about his own travels and adventures. He may have wanted to show off; he may have needed money; living in a literary *milieu*, he may have felt out of the swim, humiliated to reach the age of 22 without having any kind of a book published.

In themselves, all such desires and purposes are not merely harmless but positively useful : they can contribute enormously to the effect of a successful novel, constituting a major element in the pleasure that it gives. In each case, one could easily think of a famous example. Even so, these are secondary motivations : they can serve the novelist's basic need to please, but they are not to be confused with it. And where that primary requirement is not met, nothing can take its place.

If this were recognised more widely, there would be fewer rejections. The situation recurs constantly in which an author has good materials and good ideas, arising from such preoccupations as have just been listed, but has not coped successfully with the specific problems involved in working them up into a novel that will please. Sometimes, in a typescript that's full of miscellaneous value and interest, he has not yet created a situation in which these problems really arise: sometimes he seems hardly aware that they exist and could be important.

There is, in fact, a widespread tendency to underrate and even to ignore the specific demands made by the novel as an art-form. It is as though the aspiring novelist said to himself: "I have this particular purpose that I want to accomplish—a message to put across, a vision of life to communicate, a technique to explore. If I do *this* successfully in the medium of prose fiction, I shall have produced a workable novel." The trouble is that in certain cases, such reasoning can be valid. The born and natural story-teller, proceeding in this fashion, will in fact produce a good story, automatically and by instinct, while giving it also the extraneous and supporting power of his own preoccupations and urgencies.

But the writer less fortunate will come a cropper. His book may contain any amount of good meat, but it won't be dished up so as to tempt and then gratify the palate. He needs to apply himself to the art of cookery, remembering the old gloomy observation that "God sends the food, but the Devil sends the cooks."

And since the technological fallacy *is* a fallacy, precise instructions about the art of cookery cannot be given. There has to be experiment, with much critical and doubtful tasting and much use of the swill-bin. But the novelist can at least be advised to purify his intentions and direct his purposes. If his kitchen-work is governed by a basic and over-riding desire to please the people in the dining-room, and by a certain control and subordination of his other aspirations, he will be in a fair way to the achievement of something that may rise far above the level of mere entertainment.

He will also have some hope of pleasing the all-powerful character who now addresses him.

CHAPTER ELEVEN

JUDGMENT AND FATE

LATE AT NIGHT, perhaps, while the rain lashes at the side of the house, while the November wind moans in the chimneys, while the cat yawns and scratches her nose and curls up again on the hearthrug, the publisher's reader will come to the end of your novel. He will lay the typescript aside, and rub his poor tired eyes, and stare for a few moments at the dying fire, brooding over the whole experience that you have just conferred upon him. Then he will add a few last words and phrases to the notes that he took in the course of reading; and he'll stretch and sigh and think of bed.

The experience needs to be slept on. Even if he finishes your book in the mid-afternoon, he will very seldom sit down and type out a report on it at once : even for this very small and specialised kind of writing, experience will need to be simmered a little in the stockpot of semi-conscious memory before it's fit for serving up.

And as with your own literary notebook (if you keep one), there will only be a limited value in the various notes and jottings that he took in the course of his exploration. They may be extensive : they may cover several pages of his shorthand pad. If only to fix this particular novel very clearly in his mind—he reads a lot of novels—the reader will have jotted down an outline summary of what your novel is and how it works—a summary not primarily of the 'plot' but rather of the imaginative pattern, an idiosyncratic summary, the bones of a semi-poetic interpretation. And he will have noted down comments and observations that occurred to him at the time of reading, various apt and telling phrases that might possibly go into his report.

And some page-numbers will be individually noted: here and there, you will almost certainly have been guilty of inaccuracy or inconsistency or something of the kind. For these and similar reasons, the publisher's attention will have to be drawn to certain individual passages: some might (for example) be libellous.

These notes would mean little to you if you saw them: they are a mass of private codes and abbreviations, and doodlings, and general mess. The modern novel being what it is, I find it necessary to have a quickly-written code to denote the act of love—a filthy picture, stylised into a particular squiggle that can't mean anything else. I don't want to waste too much of my time in writing out what (in these notes) would be called 4LWs.

The grey morning comes, and there's a report to be written: possibly two, conceivably three. I find it just possible to carry three books in my head at once, without too much danger of the wires getting crossed. But a close similarity between any pair of them will make this a bit risky: two will normally be enough. And like a suitcase, the mind will have to be unpacked in the reverse order: the book that went into it first will come out of it last.

It is now the reader's task to place on record his own response to the typescript before him, his judgment upon its merit and possibilities, his recommendation as to its fate. And even in this most small and private species of literary composition, the creative mind functions as elsewhere, in a fashion empirical and experimental: the reader's judgment is crystallised by the act of writing the report. "How can I know what I think until I see what I say?'

He sits down at his typewriter, therefore, with the memory of the book very active in his mind, but not necessarily with any precise judgment and recommendation already formulated. That will emerge as he proceeds.

So he taps out the title of the book and the author's name, scowls, looks out of the window, and then embarks upon a task that is—in the first instance—descriptive and even poetic. He wants his friends in the publishing office to know what this novel is and how it works: by lyrical suggestion and evocation rather than by any detailed summary of the plot, he wants to convey, briefly but precisely, an idea of what this new reading experience is like.

He will do this sympathetically, even if the novel is quite plainly a bad and unworkable one. Assessment comes later: the thing needed at this first stage is an accurate suggestion of what commodities are here on offer, of what the author was trying to say and do and make. The nature of the attempt comes first: later on, we can ask whether the attempt was successful and whether the project was worth doing.

This part of the report will be written out of the reader's semi-conscious memory: only exceptionally, at this stage, will he have recourse to his notes. Later on, he will refer to them in connection with particular page-numbers, particular points that need attention. But there may not be any of these; and in this event, the reader's notes—so carefully taken down, with all those codes and abbreviations—may never be read at all. But they will have served their purpose, verbalising the experience (in tentative fashion) while it proceeded, fixing it in the mind and memory.

Having described and evoked the book to his own satisfaction, and in terms which will already have implied the whole drift of the report, the reader will turn to assessment. Sometimes in clear systematic fashion, but more usually by implication, he tries to suggest answers to a number of distinct questions. What (in general terms) was the author trying to do? Was it worth doing? Has he done it successfully? Has it often been done before? Did the book choose its author wisely? Can it be imagined as selling? To what kind of readership does it appeal? How are the reviewers—at various levels of brow—likely to respond? Will there be problems of libel, blasphemy, sedition, or obscenity? In general: does the thing function? And at what pressure or intensity? And how *saleably*? And finally, the reader will make something like a precise and concrete recommendation.

He formulates this within his own terms of reference. He is very seldom a director, and not always even a salaried employee, of the publishing firm in question: he makes no final decision, and he cannot accurately be said to have a vote. His report, probably taken in conjunction with others, will constitute part of the evidence upon which the final verdict is based.

This practical decision will be taken in the office: it will probably be authorised and made formal by the signature of one man, a director, but it will be reached by a more or less complicated process of discussion and voting within the firm. The nature and complexity of this process will depend upon the size of the firm and the power-system or pecking-order that prevails within it. Sometimes there will be acrimonious differences of opinion.

But however it is reached, the decision must have a clear-cut character: in the last resort, it must be a matter of a simple Yes or a simple No. There is no possible compromise between publishing a book and not publishing it. To a certain degree, therefore, the publisher and his reader are always at cross-purposes. The publisher is straining towards a moment of absolute all-or-none decision, one way or the other: the reader is trying to do justice to a literary phenomenon and a consequent practical situation that are both full of ambiguities. He will often be reproached for sitting on the fence, for hedging his bets: the publisher will say, crossly, that his recommendation was too evasively stated or too heavily qualified to be of any practical value. In such a case, the reader will retort spiritedly that he was only being frank and realistic: he will point out that there was no overwhelmingly strong case either for accepting or for rejecting this novel. "If you want me to take a practical publishing decision," he may add, "you'd better pay me a practical publishing salary." That will usually silence the grumbling business man.

But the reader wants to be helpful rather than argumentative, and his final recommendation will be as clear-cut as the facts of the matter permit. And sitting now at his desk, tapping out the last sentences of his report, he will bear in mind two facts about the publisher's trade that are sometimes forgotten by authors.

The first is that literary and commercial judgments are quite distinct. Fortunately, they often coincide in practice. Good books can usually be sold, and if not at a profit, at least not at too grievous a loss: wide sales are often the reward of genuine literary merit. There is a certain soundness in public taste, though it is not always and from all points of view reliable: best-sellers are often very good books indeed.

But cases often occur in which literary considerations point in one direction and commercial considerations in another; and by its response to such problems, the character of a publishing house is very largely determined. The reader will sometimes report that a certain novel is trash, but trash of a plainly marketable and money-spinning variety. The opposite case is quite as common: very often indeed, a novel is submitted which turns out to be perfectly sound and successful in its own way, but quite incapable of being sold in a competitive market. It may appeal to a very small minority and to nobody else; it may alienate the dominant prejudices of the age too rudely; it may resemble other published work too closely; it may be grotesquely out of fashion. Many a novel is quite unmarketable at the present day because it's precisely adapted to the literary taste of thirty years ago, or (conceivably) to the literary taste of thirty years hence. Many of my own reports conclude with the unhelpful recommendation that the publisher should accept this book eagerly, provided that he can arrange somehow to have it published in 1928.

Such consideraions add complexity and charm to the publisher's gamble; and they will serve to remind the author that many factors are involved in the practical decision. If your novel is rejected, this does not necessarily mean that the publisher and his reader consider it worthless. A novel is quite often rejected only because the firm has just accepted a very similar novel, and possibly a worse one. Other situations of the same kind occur again and again: your novel's merit is only one of the factors that will determine its fate, so far as a single publishing house is concerned.

On the whole, a reader is asked for literary rather than commercial judgments: if a publisher wants to know what can be sold, his sales manager is the man he should consult. Even so, the reader will not make a wholly abstract or ivory-tower kind of judgment and recommendation. As he writes his report, he will be considering—and checking for plausibility—an image of this messy typescript magically transformed into a bright new book, nicely printed, brightly jacketed, smelling of glue, praised by the reviewers, selling in the bookshops, preferred by many sane people to the actual money that's in their pockets, so that they buy it. And very often, even while he was enjoying the novel, it will have come home to him that this vision is grossly implausible. He knows something of the book trade, and he has to bear its limitations in mind.

He must also bear in mind the fact that a publisher deals in authors quite as much as in books. The immediate or foreground question, of course, concerns the decision to accept or reject this particular book. But this decision has to be taken in the context of a wider question, and is powerfully affected by it: the publisher is also taking the long view, and wondering whether he wants to have this author on his list as a permanent property and a long-term investment.

These two questions can affect each other in various ways, modifying a reader's recommendations accordingly. A publisher will very often be willing to accept imperfect work by a young author who shows promise; he has his faults, but he may grow out of them, and if not, it may be possible to coax and bully him out of them. This first novel of his will obviously lose money; but one can reasonably gamble on the hope that his fourth will be excellent, and publish this one in the meantime to encourage him and to get him permanently on to the firm's list. Such a gamble might be foolish, however, if the author were old and set in his ways; and a reader's report will often conclude with two alternative recommendations—acceptance as a long-term gamble if the author is young and flexibly-minded, rejection if his arteries have hardened already.

The publisher's reader will prudently retain a carbon copy of every report that he writes, filing these alphabetically under their authors' names; and he will thus be able to keep an eye on the developing career of any author—published or not—who submits successive novels to his firm. This will help him to assess a novelist's long-term prospects, as well as his present performance. Is he developing? Is he learning from his mistakes and failures? Is he writing too many books too quickly? Is he crippled by some obsession, some King Charles's head, some private lunacy? Does he repeat himself over the years? Is he in touch? Is he a spent force? Or is he perhaps blossoming out in new and unexpected directions?

An author needs to be considered in the time-dimension. The answers to such questions as these, and the consequent assessment of his future potential, may have a powerful and even a decisive bearing upon the immediate question of rejection or acceptance.

The publisher's task is a complex one, and a reader's report can be useful to him in other ways. Sometimes he will seek a report on a novel that he's already decided to accept: it's by a well-established novelist and an old friend of the firm, perhaps, and there's no real question of rejecting it. Even so, various problems will arise. This old friend's powers may be waning, and the book may be a relative failure, though still publishable: in such a case, the reader's report may point to a discreetly small print-order, as against the vast quantities of ten years ago, when she was in her prime. And in every instance, the publisher will want to have a full and precise image of what the book is, of its point and flavour, its tone of voice, its readership: this image will affect his policy in such matters as production and advertising, and the reader's contribution to it will be helpful. More is involved than the simple decision of Yes or No.

But even the most distinguished novelists are under judgment like the rest. No publisher likes to reject a book by a world-famous name or an old friend; but fashions change and powers decline, and this is sometimes necessary. Alternatively, while agreeing reluctantly to publish the book now offered, he may find it necessary to scold the author, to chide him for a wrong turning foolishly taken, to fire a warning shot across his bows. In such matters, he will often seek advice and support.

The publisher's reader is chiefly concerned with the rejection of mediocre books. But his file also bears secret unpublishable witness to great careers that were fostered, guided, corrected, and in some cases terminated by the help of his judgment.

Fully and perhaps exaggeratedly aware of his responsibility, he will come to the end of his report, making his recommendation as precise as the facts allow and making his criticisms as constructive as possible.

His report will be compact, and therefore allusive rather than explanatory. A publisher tends to be a busy man, his morning overshadowed by the impending burden of a twelve-till-three lunch; his time is much taken up with conferences and meetings, with too much business to be got through in too short a time. This novel and the reader's report will probably be considered in the course of such a meeting, and the report itself will quite possibly be read out to the assembled editorial staff : nobody will be pleased if the proceedings are held up by long literary essays. But if the reader's report contrives—within a small compass—to be entertaining as well as precise and responsible, and thus to enliven the wet-Monday-morning dullness of the office routine, the publisher may conceivably be gratified.

Some time later, when the publisher's reader has forgotten all about you, the postman will bring to your door the one thing or the other : a lovely thin envelope or a disappointing large familiar parcel. Let us hope that you get the letter, rendering you almost giddy with pleasure and excitement as you study the terms proposed. But if you get the parcel instead, and with it that short standard letter of rejection, do not despair : there are many publishers. Send the book out on its travels, send it round the houses: when it starts to look dog-eared and second-hand, re-type the first few pages and the last few pages and put it into a new file or envelope. Don't let it be too obvious to the *next* publisher's reader who sees it that this novel has already been rejected by several of his fellows. It's bound to prejudice him a little.

Rejection of any kind is always bitter, and is liable to arouse self-pity and indignation. Try to keep this under control. If your novel has been turned down, it will very seldom be wise for you to write to the publisher in the hope of having its rejection usefully explained to you; and you will be acting in a useless and tiresome fashion if you try to bully him into changing his mind.

Under the stress of disappointment, some authors display an astonishing lack of tact. "My novel may not be very good," they say, "but at least it's better than some of the infernal guff that you *do* publish!" To say this is to accuse the publisher of professional incompetence: that isn't the way to soften hearts, that isn't the way to be loved.

Try not to have any feeling of grievance towards the publisher who has rejected your novel. He's in business, and he's responsible to the shareholders or the family who own his firm: he has no duty at all towards you. Don't curse him for failing in that imagined duty. Nobody asked you to write a novel.

In these matters, some people feel strongly; and it may be desirable to clear the air by asserting, with some emphasis, the wholly gratuitous character of all activities connected with the novel. In particular, let there be no talk of 'duty'. No kind of duty comes into the picture at any point. It is not morally incumbent upon anybody to write a novel, or to write one kind of novel rather than another; no publisher has a duty to accept any particular book for publication; and nobody is to be praised or blamed for reading or for not reading, for loving or for hating, any novel at all. It's up to them.

A novelist is (among other things) a man who proposes to sell his wares in the open market. He believes that they will be in some way beneficial to the purchaser, offering him immediate enjoyment at least, and maybe some profounder benefits. But if he fails to sell his wares, he only has himself to blame.

Many novelists (but not many good novelists) take a very different view of the matter. If their work is rejected, they feel a sense of grievance : they talk sometimes as though the public had a duty of appreciating their work, and the publisher a corresponding duty of getting it into the bookshops and libraries, even at serious financial loss. Mention this factor, and they mutter darkly about 'commercialism' : they will also invoke, too often and too easily, the well-known fact that great work sometimes seems unappetising and unsaleable on its first appearance. Sometimes they go on to claim that writers ought to be subsidised by the government—in other words, that if the public are not willing to pay for their work, they should be compelled to pay for it.

That man is a poor lover who, having failed to seduce, dreams sulkily of ravishing instead.

The situation is, on the whole, a healthy one. A great many novels do get published, including some that were never likely to sell widely : most publishers do from time to time accept books that are quite certain to lose money. They do this partly for idealistic reasons, seeing themselves as the servants of Literature; but they also do it for long-term commercial reasons. In the course of time, a minority-taste can spread : your first novel may sell in hundreds only to a discerning few, your fifth in tens of thousands to the rabble. Apart from this, it's sound business for a publisher to give his firm an image of general adventurousness and receptivity : if he loses money on some remarkable book for the few, this may well be a good investment, impressing the agents, bringing him in a wider field of future choice, extending his scope generally.

There is always the possibility, of course, that some really outstanding book may fail completely to get into print and that the world may thus be impoverished, seriously and for ever. This may actually happen from time to time. But the publisher's reader, who is something of an expert on unpublished books, finds it hard to believe that it happens very often.

Generally speaking, the market is to be trusted. The publisher is certainly a business man, and he wants his firm to stay in business and make a profit if possible. But only in the lower reaches of the trade is he likely to be only a businessman, only a money-chaser. Publishing salaries are modest: if a man has sufficient energy and intelligence to hold down an editorial post in a good firm, he could almost certainly command a higher salary and an easier life in some more frankly commercial activity. But he stays in publishing because he's something of a literary idealist and also something of a gambler, studying the form but—in the last resort—backing his fancy. He also finds it fun: it *is* fun: publishing offices tend to be cheerful crazy places.

An author will sometimes suspect that his publisher is something of a *dilettante*, needing to be jollied along in such matters as sales and advertising, not quite sharp and savage enough as a business man. Authors, those remote and dreamy types, those dwellers apart in ivory towers, tend to be astonishingly fierce and businesslike where their own promotion and their own sales are concerned. They need the money, of course: as Johnson rightly said, no man but a blockhead ever wrote except for money. By comparison with these determined strivers who constitute his list, a publisher will sometimes seem a shade ineffectual. But only seldom will he lie open to any charge of mere commercialism. There are such cases, and they may be increasing in number: but to the sensitive nostrils of the writing man, they should be recognisable a mile off.

For the aspiring novelist, a certain democratic humility of mind is therefore appropriate. He can play the market without fear or scruple: if his novel has any workable kind and degree of merit, some fool will publish it. He will not be sinning against the light if he tries to please. His writing will be done, no doubt, out of some complex turmoil of inner compulsions, and he will do full justice to this, not wishing to compromise what—by a misleading analogy—he will probably call his 'artistic conscience'.

Even so, his work should have an orientation beyond himself : at the back of his mind, he should never forget the fact that he is trying to capture the attention and favour of a public—large or small, vulgar or sophisticated—that owes him nothing at all.

He needs to please them. If he fails in this, he won't be read; and his higher purposes—if he has any—won't have any chance of being fulfilled.

You have sweated blood, now, for a couple of years or more; and let us suppose that you have been successful, rewarded in the outcome with a contract and a cheque that will be spent very quickly and a certain degree of public attention. This will also go quickly. There will be a brief period during which you can cherish the illusion that everybody is talking about your newly-published novel. But it won't last. You are practising an art that's almost as ephemeral, nowadays, as journalism : within three months, your novel will be completely submerged and forgotten.

Was it worth the effort? If you have succeeded in pleasing a certain number of people, and also in earning a little money for yourself, that is no mean thing : you might easily have been employed less fruitfully, more mischievously.

But for this activity, you should not claim too grand a dignity. Story-telling is an archaic and fundamental amusement of the human race, a primitive thing, agreeable but unimportant, easily spoilt and made tedious when ultimate large burdens are placed upon it. People like stories : ever since language began, they have enjoyed telling them and listening to them. This causes some high-minded characters to raise their eyebrows at once, dismissing mere 'story' as a somewhat ape-like business, more suitable for the cave than for the cultured salon. "Neanderthal man listened to stories," says Forster, scornfully, "if one may judge by the shape of his skull." And from various other directions, belittling remarks are heard. "Novels are lies, novelists disreputable people in their basic nature," says Angus Wilson, who ought to know; "Gossip, confidence trickster, huckster, or novelist, all are kept

in action by the power of narrating." "Some very primitive factors are involved in creation," says Robert Liddell, "—in particular, cruelty. Drama is more akin to mimicry, the novel to
gossip and even scandal-mongering, than either of them is to
Science or Philosophy." Stevenson is a little kinder: "Fiction,"
he tells us, "is to the grown man what play is to the child." In
child or in kitten, play serves a very useful biological purpose.

The novel certainly has a lot in common with some very
humble activities. It thrives, for one thing, upon the mere vulgar
curiosity which most people have about what the neighbours
are doing. Among the various impulses which drive us to read
a novel, some are very closely connected with the impulse that
makes us peer over the garden fence, or even into the windows
of bedroom or bathroom. There's a kind of low pleasure in
merely being told about other people, and it doesn't depend
upon truth: when some nasty scandal goes whispering round
the suburb, we are avid to listen, and we brush aside the
reminders given by our better judgment, to the effect that the
tale is probably exaggerated or false. We want to hear it any-
way: we follow it eagerly, just as we follow newspaper-stories
about people we've never heard of before and will never hear of
again. 'Other people' may constitute Hell, as Sartre asserted;
but this Hell, if no other, is fascinating.

Of all such urges, we shall tend to be slightly ashamed: vulgar
curiosity is an ugly thing. But the version of it that is nourished
by stories can be seen in a more favourable light. "Literary
experience," says C. S. Lewis, "heals the wound, without undermining the privilege, of individuality": it enables us to escape
from the prison of self, "it admits us to experiences not our own,"
it enlarges life. It offers us an escape; and as Lewis once pointed
out, 'escapism' is only a dirty word to those who are, by instinct,
jailers.

If the idea of escapism shocks you, don't take refuge from
concrete life in either reading or writing. Put on the kettle and
fetch bandages.

But do we need to be so severe? Fiction eases the pain of our frustration and bewilderment in a difficult world. As Margaret Kennedy puts it, novel-readers "want pattern, design, order, and harmony : they want some contradiction, not of the tragedy but of the pointlessness in human existence." When we read a good novel, we are being conducted round the human landscape by somebody who seems to understand it and to be in command of things; and this will be no less truly the case if the implications of his novel are nihilistic or despairing. The nihilism, the despair will seem to be externalised, to be brought under control, to be tied down into nice safe words : the insoluble mysteries and agonies of life, by virtue of being handled and ordered in print, will lose something of their power to hurt.

By being a patterned structure, moving on to a conclusion where all knots are untied and there is rest, a good novel imposes shape upon the flux of experience, and provides a light in which things seem to make sense. If there is a God, it therefore provides us with a distant glimpse of ultimate reality : if there is no God, it offers an illusory comfort that we sorely need, and in that case, no objection can consistently be made to the pursuit of illusion. Which view you take will depend upon your view of the universe and of life.

"Those who can't, teach." This book is not written by a successful novelist, nor yet by an unsuccessful one : should you pay any attention to what it says?

Possibly not : you are on your own and (in the last resort) beyond all help. You are certainly unlikely to be helped by the great masters. Many of them have written about the novelist's art, and often in a tone of fine assured dogmatism : their words have been quoted from time to time in this book, if only to lend spurious authority to my own subjective dogmatisings. But they won't help you very much. With sound experience behind them, they may appear to say "This is how you can write a novel, this is how you *should* do it." But if you look a little closer, you will find almost invariably that they have only described their own particular practice. Each one sets forth a method, an approach that has worked for him: arrogant as the artist commonly is, he has then elevated his personal approach into a universal rule. Such rules are never to be trusted: the method or approach that works for Stendhal, for Dostoievsky, for that new fellow in Scunthorpe, may or may not work for your own improbable and unexpected self. You'll have to try; you'll have to find your own way. Meanwhile, the world goes about its affairs and owes you nothing: not even attention.

The publisher's reader lives in a valley of dry bones: novels to left of him, novels to right of him stagger and crumble: failure is in the atmosphere that he breathes. He has sat by many a literary deathbed, he has diagnosed many a terminal case: his gentle loving heart is full of compassion. If you want his personal advice—you are, after all, a close friend and a very dear person —he will tell you not to do it. That letter of rejection hurts: most novelists receive it: he doesn't want to see you bleeding.

All lies, all lies. What does he care about your suffering? He still nurses the unconquerable hope. Get to work!

Tomorrow he will look for the first time upon some new novel, a clean typescript, two hundred and twenty-three pages on quarto paper, bound up in some tiresome fashion. But it's your first novel, and I guarantee that his heart will be full of joyous expectation. This is going to be the real thing.